3 00?? 00556141 8

TRUE ROMANCE

W/O

D1188637

by the same author

RESERVOIR DOGS
PULP FICTION

TRUE ROMANCE

Quentin Tarantino

faber and faber
LONDON · BOSTON

812 TAR 350474.

First published in Great Britain in 1995
by Faber and Faber Limited
3 Queen Square London WC1N 3AU

Photoset by Parker Typesetting Service, Leicester
Printed in England by Clays Ltd, St Ives plc

All rights reserved

© Quentin Tarantino, 1995
Photos from *True Romance* © BFI Stills, Posters and Designs

*This book is sold subject to the condition that it shall not, by way of trade
or otherwise, be lent, resold, hired out or otherwise circulated without the
publisher's prior consent in any form of binding or cover other than that
in which it is published and without a similar condition including
this condition being imposed on the subsequent purchaser.*

A CIP record for this book
is available from the British Library

ISBN 0-571-17593-7

2 4 6 8 10 9 7 5 3

'His films are a desperate cry from the heart of a grotesque fast-food culture.'
                                    – French critics on the films of Roger Corman

'. . . Beyond all the naïveté and stupidity, beyond the vulgarity inherent in the amount of money involved, beyond all this, a certain grandeur had rooted itself into the scheme, and I could still spy a reckless and artistic splendour to the way we had carried it out.'
                                    – Clifford Irving on the Howard Hughes hoax

INTRODUCTION

Quentin Tarantino on:

BEGINNINGS

The first script I ever did was *True Romance*. I wrote it to do the way
the Coen brothers did *Blood Simple*, and I almost directed it. Me
and a friend, Roger Avary, were going to raise about $1.2 million,
form a limited partnership and then go off and make the movie. We
worked on it for three years, trying to get it off the ground like that,
and it never worked. I then wrote *Natural Born Killers*, again hoping
to direct it myself, this time for half a million dollars – I was shooting
lower and lower. After a year and a half I was no further along than
at the beginning. It was then, out of frustration, that I wrote
Reservoir Dogs. I was going to go really guerrilla-style with it, like the
way Nick Gomez did *Laws of Gravity*. I'd lost faith in anyone giving
me money – and then that's *when* I got the money.

After *Reservoir Dogs* I was offered both of them to direct. The
producers who had *Natural Born Killers* – before Oliver Stone
acquired it – tried like hell to talk me into directing it. Tony Scott
and Bill Unger had *True Romance*. I had convinced Tony to direct it,
but Bill was saying, 'Look, Quentin, would you be interested in
doing this as a follow-up to *Reservoir Dogs*?' And my answer was no.
I didn't want to do either one of them because they were both
written to be my first film and by then I'd made my first film. I
didn't want to go backwards and do old stuff. I think of them as old
girlfriends: I loved them, but I didn't want to marry them any more.
The thing that I am happiest about is that the first film of mine
produced was one that I directed.

STRUCTURE

True Romance had a complicated structure to start with, but when
the producers bought the script, they cut-and-pasted it into a linear
form. The original structure was also an answers-first, questions-
later structure, like *Reservoir Dogs*. Tony Scott actually started
putting it together that way in the editing room, but he said it didn't
work for him. I guess what I'm always trying to do is use these
structures that I see in novels and apply them to cinema. A novelist
thinks nothing of starting in the middle of a story. I thought that if

you could figure out a cinematic way to do that, it would be very exciting. Generally, when they translate novels to movies, that's the first stuff that goes out. I don't do this to be a wise guy or to show how clever I am. If a story would be more dramatically engaging if it were told from the beginning, or the end, then I'd tell it that way. But the *glory* is in pulling it off my way.

OMISSION

What you leave out is as crucial as what you put in. To me, omission even applies to the way you frame a shot. What you don't see in the frame is as important as what you do see. Some people like to show everything. They don't want the audience to have a second guess about anything; it's *all* there. I'm not like that. I've seen so many movies that I like playing around with them. Pretty much nine out of ten movies you see let you know in the first ten minutes what kind of movie it's going to be, and I think the audience subconsciously reads this early ten-minute message and starts leaning to the left when the movie is getting ready to make a left turn; they're predicting what the movie is going to do. And what I like to do is use that information against them. *Natural Born Killers* opens with a lazy coffee-shop scene that suddenly turns into a massacre. In *True Romance*, Alabama has a terrifying fight with a hit man. One of the reasons that I think that that scene is so exciting is because dramatically, in the context of where it falls in the movie, Alabama could get killed. We like Alabama, but it's getting towards the end of the movie and it would make a lot of sense for her to die. It would give Clarence something to do for the last fifteen minutes – avenge her.

I once saw this Stephen King movie called *Silver Bullet*, with Gary Busey. It's got this little kid in a wheelchair and this young girl who's narrating the story. At the end, there's a big fight with a werewolf – and I was so scared for Gary Busey! I knew they weren't going to kill the little kid in the wheelchair or the girl because she's the narrator, but Gary Busey *could* die. Dramatically, they could have killed him – and so it was really scary. My sympathy was with him, because he was perishable. The point is, I didn't know what was going to happen.

HEROES *and* VILLAINS

Throughout *True Romance*, Clarence and Alabama keep running into all these people, and when they do, the movie becomes the story of the people they meet. When they're with Clarence's father, I treat him as though the whole movie is going to be about him. When Vicenzo Coccotti, the gangster that Christopher Walken plays, comes in, the whole movie could be about him. The same thing with Drexl, the Gary Oldman character. But particularly the father – you just figure he's going to play a central role. One of the things I don't like about comedy-action films is comic villains. They're never a threat; they're usually just buffoonish. The villains in *True Romance* rub Dennis Hopper out. That's a shock. All right – so now these guys are really, really scary, and every time they come in you think the worst thing in the world could happen.

VIOLENCE

I don't take the violence very seriously. I find violence very funny, especially in the stories that I've been telling recently. Violence is part of this world and I am drawn to the outrageousness of real-life violence. It isn't about people lowering people from helicopters on to speeding trains, or about terrorists hijacking something or other. Real-life violence is, you're in a restaurant and a man and his wife are having an argument and all of a sudden that guy gets so mad at her, he picks up a fork and stabs her in the face. That's really crazy and comic bookish – but it also *happens*; that's how real violence comes kicking and screaming into your perspective in real life. I am interested in the act, in the explosion, and in the entire aftermath of that. What do we do after this? Do we beat up the guy who stabbed the woman? Do we separate them? Do we call the cops? Do we ask for our money back because our meal has been ruined? I am interested in answering all those questions.

To me, violence is a totally aesthetic subject. Saying you don't like violence in movies is like saying you don't like dance sequences in movies. I do like dance sequences in movies, but if I didn't, it doesn't mean I should stop dance sequences being made. When you're doing violence in movies, there's going to be a lot of people who aren't going to like it, because it's a mountain they can't climb. And they're not *jerks*. They're just not into that. And they don't *have* to be into it. There's other things that they can see. If you *can* climb that mountain, then I'm going to give you something to climb.

ix

MORALITY

I'm not trying to preach any kind of morals or get any kind of message across, but for all the wildness that happens in my movies, I think that they usually lead to a moral conclusion. For example, I find what passes between Mr White and Mr Orange at the end of *Reservoir Dogs* very moving and profound in its morality and its human interaction.

ENDINGS

In my original script, Clarence gets killed. If I were to write a script and sell it now, I would make the provision that they wouldn't change anything. I can do that now, but at the time I was selling *True Romance* to get the money to make *Reservoir Dogs* it never occurred to me it would get changed. When I read the new ending, in which Clarence survives, I felt that it worked – I just didn't think it was as good an ending as mine. My ending has a symmetry with the whole piece. At first, I was really distraught about it; in fact, I was talking about taking my name off the film. I had a lot of faith in Tony Scott – I'm a big fan of his work, especially *Revenge* – but where I was coming from, you just couldn't change my ending.

Anyway, we got together and talked about it, and Tony said that he wanted to change the ending in particular, not for commercial reasons, but because he really liked these kids and he wanted to see them get away. He said, 'Quentin, I'm going to defer to you. I'm going to shoot both endings, then I'm going to look at them, and then decide which one I want to go with.' As much as I didn't want my ending changed, I figured I couldn't really ask for more than that. When it came to it, he really liked the happy ending and went with it.

CODA

True Romance is probably my most personal script because the character of Clarence was me at the time I wrote it. He works at a comic book shop – I was working in a video store. When my friends from that time see *True Romance*, they get melancholy; it brings back a certain time for us. It was weird when I first saw the movie because it was like looking at a big-budget version of my home movies, or memories.

True Romance

When you're tired of relationships,
try a romance.

Clarence (Christian Slater)

Alabama (Patricia Arquette)

True Romance was released in 1993.

The cast included:

CLARENCE WORLEY	Christian Slater
ALABAMA WHITMAN	Patricia Arquette
CLIFFORD WORLEY	Dennis Hopper
MENTOR (ELVIS)	Val Kilmer
DREXL SPIVEY	Gary Oldman
FLOYD	Brad Pitt
VINCENZO COCCOTTI	Christopher Walken
ELLIOT BLITZER	Bronson Pinchot
BIG DON	Samuel L. Jackson
DICK RITCHIE	Michael Rapaport
NICKY DIMES	Chris Penn
CODY NICHOLSON	Tom Sizemore

Written by	Quentin Tarantino
Directed by	Tony Scott
Produced by	Bill Unger
	Steve Perry
	Samuel Hadida
Director of Photography	Jeffrey L. Kimball
Art Director	James J. Murakami
Costume Design	Susan Becker
Editors	Michael Tronick
	Christian Wagner
Music	Hans Zimmer

A Morgan Creek production
Released through Warner Bros.

INT. BAR – NIGHT

A smoky cocktail bar in downtown Detroit.

Clarence Worley, a young hipster hepcat, is trying to pick up on an older lady named Lucy. She isn't bothered by him, in fact, she's a little charmed. But, you can tell that she isn't going to leave her barstool.

CLARENCE

In 'Jailhouse Rock' he's everything rockabilly's about. I mean, he is rockabilly: mean, surly, nasty, rude. In that movie he couldn't give a fuck about anything except rockin' and rollin', livin' fast, dyin' young, and leaving a good-lookin' corpse. I love that scene where after he's made it big he's throwing a big cocktail party, and all these highbrows are there, and he's singing, 'Baby You're So Square . . . Baby, I Don't Care.' Now, they got him dressed like a dick. He's wearing these stupid-lookin' pants, this horrible sweater. Elvis ain't no sweater boy. I even think they got him wearin' penny loafers. Despite all that shit, all the highbrows at the party, big house, the stupid clothes, he's still a rude-lookin' motherfucker. I'd watch that hillbilly and I'd want to be him so bad. Elvis looked good. I'm no fag, but Elvis was good-lookin'. He was fuckin' prettier than most women. I always said if I ever had to fuck a guy . . . I mean *had* too 'cause my life depended on it . . . I'd fuck Elvis.

Lucy takes a drag from her cigarette.

LUCY

I'd fuck Elvis.

CLARENCE

Really?

LUCY

When he was alive. I wouldn't fuck him now.

CLARENCE

I don't blame you.

5

(*they laugh*)
So we'd both fuck Elvis. It's nice to meet people with common interests, isn't it?

Lucy laughs.

Well, enough about the King, how 'bout you?

                    LUCY
How 'bout me what?

                    CLARENCE
How 'bout you go to the movies with me tonight?

                    LUCY
What are we gonna go see?

                    CLARENCE
A Sonny Chiba triple feature. *The Streetfighter*, *Return of the Streetfighter*, and *Sister Streetfighter*.

                    LUCY
Who's Sonny Chiba?

                    CLARENCE
He is, bar none, the greatest actor working in martial arts movies ever.

                    LUCY
                (*not believing this*)
You wanna take me to a kung fu movie?

                    CLARENCE
                (*holding up three fingers*)
Three kung fu movies.

Lucy takes a drag from her cigarette.

                    LUCY
                (*laughing*)
I don't think so. Not my cup of tea.

TITLE SEQUENCE

TITLE CARD:
                    'MOTORCITY'

6

INT. DINGY HOTEL ROOM – DAY

The sounds of the city flow in through an open window: car horns, gun shots and voices. Paint is peeling off the walls and the once green carpet is stained black.

On the bed nearby is a huge open suitcase filled with clear plastic bags of cocaine. Shotguns and pistols have been dropped carelessly around the suitcase. On the far end of the room, against the wall, is a TV.
Bewitched *is playing.*

At the opposite end of the room, by the front door, is a table. Drexl Spivey and Floyd Dixon sit around it. Cocaine is on the table as well as little plastic bags and a weigher. Floyd is black, Drexl is a white boy, though you wouldn't know it to listen to him.

> DREXL

Nigger, get outta my face with that bullshit.

> FLOYD

Naw man, I don't be eatin' that shit.

> DREXL

That's bullshit.

Big Don Watts, a stout, mean-looking black man who's older than Drexl and Floyd, walks through the door carrying hamburgers and french fries in two greasy brown-paper bags.

> FLOYD

Naw man that's some serious shit.

> DREXL

Nigger, you lie like a big dog.

> BIG D

What the fuck are you talkin' about?

> DREXL

Floyd say he don't be eatin' pussy.

> BIG D

Shit, any nigger say he don't eat pussy is lyin' his ass off.

                              DREXL
I heard that.

                              FLOYD
Hold on a second, Big D. You sayin' you eat pussy?

                              BIG D
Nigger, I eat everything. I eat the pussy. I eat the butt. I eat every
motherfuckin' thang.

                              DREXL
Preach on, Big D.

                              FLOYD
Looky here. If I ever did eat some pussy – I would never eat any
pussy – but, if I did eat some pussy, I sure as hell wouldn't tell no
goddamn body. I'd be ashamed as a motherfucker.

                              BIG D
Shit! Nigger, you smoke enough sherm your dumb ass'll do a lot a
crazy ass things. So you won't eat pussy? Motherfucker, you'll be
up there suckin' niggers' dicks.

                              DREXL
Heard that.

Drexl and Big D bump fists.

                              FLOYD
Yeah, that's right, laugh. It's so funny oh it's so funny.
                    (*he takes a hit off of a joint*)
There used to be a time when sisters didn't know shit about gettin'
their pussy licked. Then the sixties came an' they started fuckin'
around with white boys. And white boys are freaks for that shit –

                              DREXL
– Because it's good!

                              FLOYD
Then, after a while sisters get use to gettin' their little pussy eat.
And because you white boys had to make pigs of yourselves, you
fucked it up for every nigger in the world everywhere.

                                8

BIG D
(*solemnly*)
Drexl. On behalf of me and all the brothers who aren't here, I'd like to express our gratitude –

Drexl and Big D bust up.

FLOYD
Go on, pussy-eaters . . . laugh. You look like you be eatin' pussy. You got pussy-eatin' mugs. Now if a nigger wants to get his dick sucked he's got to do a bunch of fucked-up shit.

BIG D
So you do eat pussy!

FLOYD
Naw naw!

BIG D
You don't like it but you eat that shit.
(*to Drexl*)
He eats it.

DREXL
Damn skippy. He like it, too.

BIG D
(*mock English accent*)
Me thinketh he doth protest too much.

FLOYD
Well fuck you guys, then! You guys are fucked up!

DREXL
Why you trippin'? We jus' fuckin' with ya. But I wanna ask you a question. You with some fine bitch, I mean a brick shithouse bitch – you're with Jayne Kennedy. You're with Jayne Kennedy and you say, 'Bitch, suck my dick!' And then Jayne Kennedy says, 'First things first, nigger, I ain't suckin' shit till you bring your ass over here an' lick my bush!' Now, what do you say?

FLOYD
I tell Jayne Kennedy, 'Suck my dick or I'll beat your ass!'

BIG D

Nigger, get real. You touch Jayne Kennedy she'll have you ass in Wayne County so fast –

DREXL

Nigger, back off, you ain't beatin' shit. Now what would you do?

FLOYD

I'd say fuck it!

Drexl and Big D get up from the table disgusted and walk away, leaving Floyd sitting all alone.

Big D sits on the bed, his back turned to Floyd, watching Bewitched.

FLOYD
(*yelling after them*)

Ain't no man have to eat pussy!

BIG D
(*not even looking*)

Take that shit somewhere else.

DREXL
(*marching back*)

You tell Jayne Kennedy to fuck it?

FLOYD

If it came down to who eats who, damn skippy.

DREXL

With that terrible mug of yours if Jayne Kennedy told you to eat her pussy, kiss her ass, lick her feet, chow on her shit, and suck her dogs dick, nigger, you'd aim to please.

BIG D
(*glued to TV*)

I'm hip.

DREXL

In fact, I'm gonna show you what I mean with a little demonstration. Big D, toss me that shotgun.

Without turning away from Bewitched *he picks up the shotgun and tosses it to Drexl.*

> DREXL
> (*to Floyd*)
> All right, check this out.
>> (*referring to shotgun*)
> Now, pretend this is Jayne Kennedy. And you're you.

Then, in a blink, he points the shotgun at Floyd and blows him away.

Big D leaps off the bed and spins toward Drexl.

Drexl, waiting for him, fires from across the room.

The blast hits the big man in the right arm and shoulder, spinning him around.

Drexl makes a beeline for his victim and fires again.

Big D is hit with a blast, full in the back. He slams into the wall and drops.

Drexl collects the suitcase full of cocaine and leaves. As he gets to the front door he surveys the carnage, spits, and walks out.

EXT. CLIFF'S MOVING CAR – MORNING

A big white Chevy Nova is driving down the road with a sunrise sky as a backdrop. The song 'Little Bitty Tear' is heard a cappella.

INT. CLIFF'S MOVING CAR – MORNING

Clifford Worley is driving his car home from work, singing this song gently to the sunrise. He's a forty-five-years-old ex-cop, at present a security guard. In between singing he takes sips from a cup of take-out coffee. He's dressed in a security guard uniform.

EXT. TRAILER PARK – MORNING

Cliff's Nova pulls in as he continues crooning. He pulls up to his trailer to see something that stops him short.

Cliff's POV through windshield.

Clarence and a nice-looking Young Woman are waiting for him in front of his trailer.

CU – Cliff

Upon seeing Clarence, a little bitty tear rolls down Cliff's cheek.

BACK TO: POV

Clarence and the Young Woman walk over to the car. Clarence sticks his face through the driver's side window.

> CLARENCE
> Good morning, Daddy. Long time no see.

INT. TRAILER HOME – MORNING

All three enter the trailer home.

> CLIFF
> Excuse the place, I haven't been entertaining company as of late. Sorry if I'm acting a little dense, but you're the last person in the world I expected to see this morning.

Clarence and the Young Girl walk into the living room.

> CLARENCE
> Yeah, well, tha's OK, Daddy, I tend to have that effect on people. I'm dyin' of thirst, you got anything to drink?

He moves past Cliff and heads straight for his refrigerator.

> CLIFF
> I think there's a Seven-Up in there.

> CLARENCE
> (*rumaging around the fridge*)
> Anything stronger?
> (*pause*)
> Oh, probably not. Beer? You can drink beer, can't you?

> CLIFF
> I can, but I don't.

> CLARENCE
> (*closing the fridge*)
> That's about all I ever eat.

Cliff looks at the girl. She smiles sweetly at him.

CLIFF
(*to girl*)

I'm sorry . . . I'm his father.

YOUNG GIRL
(*sticking her hand out*)

That's OK, I'm his wife.
(*shaking his hand vigorously*)

Alabama Worley, pleased to meetcha.

She is really pumping his arm, just like a used-car salesman. However, that's where the similarities end; Alabama's totally sincere.

Clarence steps back into the living room, holding a bunch of little ceramic fruit magnets in his hand. He throws his other arm around Alabama.

CLARENCE

Oh yeah, we got married.
(*referring to the magnets*)

You still have these!
(*to Alabama*)

This isn't a complete set; when I was five I swallowed the pomegranate one. I never shit it out, so I guess it's still there. Loverdoll, why don't you be a sport and go get us some beer. I want some beer.
(*to Cliff*)

Do you want some beer? Well, if you want some it's here.

He hands her some money and his car keys.

Go to the liquor store –
(*to Cliff*)

Where is there a liquor store around here?

CLIFF

Uh, yeah . . . there's a party store down 54th.

CLARENCE
(*to Alabama*)

Get a six-pack of something imported. It's hard to tell you what to get 'cause different places have different things. If they got Fosters, get that, if not ask the guy at the thing what the strongest imported beer he has is. Look, since you're making a beer run,

13

would you mind too terribly if you did a food run as well. I'm fuckin' starvin' to death. Are you hungry too?

ALABAMA

I'm pretty hungry. When I went to the store I was gonna get some Ding-Dongs.

CLARENCE

Well, fuck that shit, we'll get some real food. What would taste good?
(*to Cliff*)
What do you think would taste good?

CLIFF

I'm really not very –

CLARENCE

You know what would taste good? Chicken. I haven't had chicken in a while. Chicken would really hit the spot about now. Chicken and beer, definitely, absolutely, without a doubt.
(*to Cliff*)
Where's a good chicken place around here?

CLIFF

I really don't know.

CLARENCE

You don't know the chicken places around where you live?
(*to Alabama*)
Ask the guy at the place where a chicken place is.

He gives her some more money.

This should cover it, Auggie-Doggie.

ALABAMA

Okee-dokee, Doggie-Daddy.

She opens the door and starts out. Clarence turns to his dad as the door shuts.

CLARENCE

Isn't she the sweetest goddamned girl you ever saw in your whole life? Is she a four alarm fire, or what?

14

CLIFF

She seems very nice.

CLARENCE

Daddy. Nice isn't the word. Nice is an insult. She's a peach.
That's the only word for it, she's a peach. She even tastes like a
peach. You can tell I'm in love with her. You can tell by my face,
can't ya? It's a dead giveaway. It's written all over it.

Ya know what? She loves me back. Take a seat, Pop, we gotta
talk –

CLIFF

Clarence, just shut up, you're giving me a headache! I can't
believe how much like your mother you are. You're your fucking
mother through and through. I haven't heard from ya in three
years. Then ya show up all of a sudden at eight o'clock in the
morning. You walk in like a goddamn bulldozer . . . don't get me
wrong, I'm happy to see you . . . just slow it down. Now, when
did you get married?

CLARENCE

Daddy, I'm in big fuckin' trouble and I really need your help.

BLACK TITLE CARD:
'HOLLYWOOD'

INT. OUTSIDE OF CASTING DIRECTOR'S OFFICE – DAY

*Four Young Actors are sitting on a couch with sheets of paper in their
hands silently mouthing lines. One of the actors is Dick Ritchie. The
casting director, Mary Louise Ravencroft, steps into the waiting room,
clipboard in hand.*

RAVENCROFT

Dick Ritchie?

Dick pops up from the pack.

DICK

I'm me . . . I mean, that's me.

RAVENCROFT

Step inside.

15

INT. CASTING DIRECTOR'S OFFICE – DAY

She sits behind a large desk. Her name-plate rests on the desktop. Several posters advertising The Return of T. J. Hooker *hang on the wall.*

Dick sits in a chair, holding his sheets in his hands.

>   RAVENCROFT
> Well, the part you're reading for is one of the bad guys. There's Brian and Marty. Peter Breck's already been cast as Brian. And you're reading for the part of Marty. Now in this scene you're both in a car and Bill Shatner's hanging on the hood. And what you're trying to do is get him off.
>   (*she picks up a copy of the script*)
> Whenever your ready.

>   DICK
>   (*reading and miming driving*)
> Where'd he come from?

>   RAVENCROFT
>   (*reading from the script lifelessly*)
> I don't know. He just appeared like magic.

>   DICK
>   (*reading from script*)
> Well, don't just sit there, shoot him.

She puts her script down, and smiles at him.

>   RAVENCROFT
> That was very good.

>   DICK
> Thank you.

>   RAVENCROFT
> If we decided on making him a New York type, could you do that?

>   DICK
> Sure. No problem.

>   RAVENCROFT
> Could we try it now?

DICK

Absolutely.

Dick picks up the script and begins, but this time with a Brooklyn accent.

Where'd he come from?

RAVENCROFT
(*monotone, as before*)
I don't know. He just appeared like magic.

DICK

Well, don't just sit there, shoot him.

Ravencroft puts her script down.

RAVENCROFT

Well, Mr Ritchie, I'm impressed. You're a very fine actor.

Dick smiles.

INT. TRAILER HOME – DAY

Cliff's completely aghast. He just stares, unable to come to grips with what Clarence has told him.

CLARENCE

Look, I know this is pretty heavy-duty, so if you wanna explode, feel free.

CLIFF

You're always makin' jokes. That's what you do, isn't it? Make jokes. Makin' jokes is the one thing you're good at, isn't it? But if you make a joke about this –
(*raising his voice*)
– I'm gonna go completely out of my fuckin' head!

Cliff pauses and collects himself.

What do you want from me?

CLARENCE

What?

CLIFF

Stop acting like an infant. You're here because you want me to help you in some way. What do you need from me? You need money?

CLARENCE

Do you still have friends on the force?

CLIFF

Yes, I still have friends on the force.

CLARENCE

Could you find out if they know anythin'? I don't think they know shit about us. But I don't wanna *think*, I wanna *know*. You could find out for sure what's goin' on.
(*pause*)
Daddy?

CLIFF

What makes you think I could do that?

CLARENCE

You were a cop.

CLIFF

What makes you think I would do that?

CLARENCE

I'm your son.

CLIFF

You got it all worked out, don't you?

CLARENCE

Look, goddamnit, I never asked you for a goddamn thing! I've tried to make your parental obligation as easy as possible. After Mom divorced you, did I ever ask you for anything? When I wouldn't see ya for six months to a year at a time, did I ever get in your shit about it? No! It was always: 'OK,' 'no problem,' 'you're a busy guy, I understand.' The whole time you were a drunk, did I ever point my finger at you and talk shit? No! Everybody else did. I never did. You see, I know that you're just a bad parent. You're not really very good at it. But I know you love me. I'm basically a pretty resourceful guy. If I didn't really need it I wouldn't ask. And if you say no, don't worry about it. I'm gone. No problems.

Alabama walks in through the door carrying a shopping bag.

                    ALABAMA
The forager's back.

                    CLARENCE
Thank God. I could eat a horse if you slap enough catsup on it.

                    ALABAMA
I didn't get any chicken.

                    CLARENCE
How come?

                    ALABAMA
It's nine o'clock in the morning. Nothing's open.

INT. TRAILER HOME – BEDROOM – DAY

Cliff's on the telephone in his bedroom, pacing as he talks. The living room of the trailer can be seen from his doorway, where Clarence and Alabama are horsing around. They giggle and cut up throughout the scene. As Cliff talks, all the noise and hubbub of a police station comes through over the line. He's talking to Detective Wilson, an old friend of his from the force.

We see both sides of the conversation.

                    CLIFF
It's about that pimp that was shot a couple of days ago, Drexl Spivey.

                    DETECTIVE WILSON
What about him?

                    CLIFF
Well, Ted, to tell you the truth, I found out through the grapevine that it might be, and I only said *might* be, the Drexl Spivey that was responsible for that restaurant break-in on Riverdale.

                                WILSON
Are you still working security for Foster & Langley?

                                 CLIFF
Yeah, and the restaurant's on my route. And you know I stuck my
nose in for the company to try to put a stop to some of these
break-ins. Now, while I have no proof, the name Drexl Spivey
kept comin' up. Who's case is it?

                                WILSON
McTeague.

                                 CLIFF
I don't know him. Is he a nice guy? You think he'll help me out?

                                WILSON
I don't see why not. When you gonna come round and see my new
place?

                                 CLIFF
You and Robin moved?

                                WILSON
Shit, you are behind. Me and Rob got a divorce six months ago.
Got myself a new place – mirrors all over the bedroom, ceiling fans
above the bed. Guy'd have to look as ugly as King Kong not to get
laid in that place. I'm serious, a guy'd have to look like a gorilla.

CUT TO:

EXT. TRAILER HOME – DAY

*Clarence and Cliff stand by Clarence's 1965 red Mustang. Alabama is
amusing herself by doing cartwheels and handstands in the background.*

                                 CLIFF
They have nothing. In fact, they think it's drug related.

                               CLARENCE
Do tell. Why drug related?

                                 CLIFF
Apparently, Drexl had his big toe stuck in shit like that.

                                  20

CLARENCE

No shit?

CLIFF

Yeah. Drexl had an association with a fella named Blue Lou
Boyle. Name mean anything to you?

CLARENCE

Nope.

CLIFF

If you don't hang around his circle, no reason it should.

CLARENCE

Who is he?

CLIFF

Gangster. Drug dealer. Somebody you don't want on your ass.
Look, Clarence, the more I hear about this Drexl fucker, the more
I think you did the right thing. That guy wasn't just some wild
flake.

CLARENCE

That's what I've been tellin' ya. The guy was like a mad dog. So
the cops aren't lookin' for me?

CLIFF

Naw, until they hear something better they'll assume Drexl and
Blue Lou had a falling out. So, once you leave town I wouldn't
worry about it.

Clarence sticks his hand out to shake. Cliff takes it.

CLARENCE

Thanks a lot, Daddy. You really came through for me.

CLIFF

I got some money I can give you –

CLARENCE

Keep it.

CLIFF

Well, son, I want you to know I hope everything works out with
you and Alabama. I like her. I think you make a cute couple.

CLARENCE
We do make a cute couple, don't we?

CLIFF
Yeah, well, just stay outta trouble. Remember, you got a wife to think about now. Quit fuckin' around.
(*pause*)
I love you, son.

They hug each other.

Clarence takes a piece of paper out and puts it into Cliff's hand.

CLARENCE
This is Dick's number in Hollywood. We don't know where we'll be, but you can get a hold of me through him.

Clarence turns toward Alabama and yells to her.

Bama, we're outta here. Kiss Pops goodbye.

Alabama runs across from where she was and throws her arms around Cliff and gives him a big smackeroo on the lips. Cliff's a little startled. Alabama's bubbling like a Fresca.

ALABAMA
Bye, Daddy! Hope to see you again real soon.

CLARENCE
(*mock anger*)
What kind of daughterly smackeroo was that?

ALABAMA
Oh, hush up.

The two get into the Mustang.

CLARENCE
(*to Cliff*)
We'll send you a postcard as soon as we get to Hollywood.

Clarence starts the engine. The convertible roof opens as they talk.

CLIFF
Bama, you take care of that one for me. Keep him out of trouble.

22

ALABAMA

Don't worry, Daddy, I'm keepin' this fella on a short leash.

Clarence, slowly, starts driving away.

CLARENCE
(*to Cliff*)

As the sun sets slowly in the west we bid a fond farewell to all the friends we've made . . . and, with a touch of melancholy, we look forward to the time when we will all be together again.

Clarence peels out, shooting a shower of gravel up in the air.

As the Mustang disappears Cliff runs his tongue over his lips.

CLIFF

The son of a bitch was right . . . she does taste like a peach.

INT. DICK'S APARTMENT – DAY

Dick's apartment is standard issue for a young actor. Things are pretty neat and clean. A nice stereo unit sits on the shelf. A framed picture of a ballet dancer's feet hangs on the wall.

The phone rings, Dick answers.

DICK

Hi, Dick here.

INT. HOTEL SUITE – LAS VEGAS – SUNSET

Top floor, Las Vegas, Nevada hotel room with a huge picture window overlooking the neon-filled strip and the flaming red and orange sunset sky.

Clarence paces up and down with the telephone in his hand.

CLARENCE
(*big bopper voice*)

Heeeellllloooo baaaabbbbbyyyy!!

NOTE: *We intercut both sides of the conversation.*

                         DICK
                       (*unsure*)
Clarence?

                       CLARENCE
You got it.

                         DICK
It's great to hear from you.

                       CLARENCE
Well, you're gonna be seein' me shortly.

                         DICK
You comin' to LA? When?

                       CLARENCE
Tomorrow.

                         DICK
What's up? Why're ya leavin' Detroit?

*Clarence sits down on the hotel room bed. Alabama, wearing only a long
T-shirt with a big picture of Bullwinkle on it, crawls behind him.*

                       CLARENCE
Well, there's a story behind all that. I'll tell you when I see you.
By the way, I won't be alone. I'm bringin' my wife with me.

                         DICK
Get the fuck outta here!

                       CLARENCE
I'm a married man.

                         DICK
Get the fuck outta here!

                       CLARENCE
Believe it or not, I actually tricked a girl into falling in love with
me. I'm not quite sure how I did it. I'd hate to have to do it again.
But I did it. Wanna say hi to my better half?

Before Dick can respond Clarence puts Alabama on the phone.

                          24

ALABAMA

Hi, Dick. I'm Alabama Worley.

DICK

Hello, Alabama.

ALABAMA

I can't wait to meet you. Clarence told me all about you. He said you were his best friend. So, I guess that makes you my best friend, too.

Clarence starts dictating to her what to say.

CLARENCE

Tell him we gotta go.

ALABAMA

Clarence says we gotta be hittin' it.

DICK

What?

CLARENCE

Tell him we'll be hittin' his area some time tomorrow.

ALABAMA

He said don't go nowhere. We'll be there some time tomorrow.

DICK

Wait a minute –

CLARENCE

Tell him not to eat anything. We're gonna scarf when we get there.

ALABAMA

Don't eat anything.

DICK

Alabama, could you tell Clar –

CLARENCE

Ask him if he got the letter.

ALABAMA

Did you get the letter?

DICK

What letter?

ALABAMA
(*to Clarence*)

What letter?

CLARENCE

The letter I sent.

ALABAMA
(*to Dick*)

The letter he sent.

DICK

Clarence sent a letter?

CLARENCE

Has he gotten his mail today?

ALABAMA

Gotten your mail yet?

DICK

Yeah, my room-mate leaves it on the TV.

ALABAMA
(*to Clarence*)

Yes.

CLARENCE

Has he looked through it yet?

ALABAMA
(*to Dick*)

Ya looked through it?

DICK

Not yet.

ALABAMA
(*to Clarence*)

Nope.

                    CLARENCE
Tell him to look through it.

                    ALABAMA
                    (*to Dick*)
Get it.

                    DICK
Let me speak to Clarence.

                    ALABAMA
                    (*to Clarence*)
He wants to speak with you.

                    CLARENCE
No time. Gotta go. Just tell him to read the letter, the letter explains all. Tell him I love him. And tell him, as of tomorrow, all his money problems are over.

                    ALABAMA
                    (*to Dick*)
He can't. We gotta go, but he wants you to read the letter. The letter explains all. He wants you to know he loves you. And he wants you to know that as of tomorrow, all of your money problems are over.

                    DICK
Money problems?

                    CLARENCE
Now tell him goodbye.

                    ALABAMA
Bye, bye.

                    CLARENCE
Now hang up.

She hangs up the phone.

INT. DICK'S APARTMENT – DAY

Dick hears the click on the other end.

Hello, hello. Clarence? Clarence's wife? . . . I mean Alabama . . .
hello?

*Extremely confused. Dick hangs up the phone. He goes over to the TV
and picks up the day's mail. He goes through it.*

BILL: *Southern California Gas Company.*

BILL: *Group W.*

BILL: *Fossenkemp Photography.*

BILL: *Columbia Record and Tape Club.*

LETTER: *It's obviously from Clarence. Addressed to Dick. Dick opens it.*

EXT. TRAILER PARK — DAY

*A lower-middle-class trailer park named Astro World, which has a neon
sign in front of it in the shape of a planet.*

*A big, white Chevy Nova pulls into the park. It parks by a trailer that's
slightly less kept up than the others. Cliff gets out of the Chevy. He's
drinking out of a fast-food soda cup as he opens the door to his trailer.*

INT. TRAILER — DAY

*He steps inside his doorway and then, before he knows it, a gun is pressed
to his temple and a big hand grabs his shoulder.*

GUN CARRIER (DARIO)
Welcome home, alchy. We're havin' a party.

*Cliff is roughly shoved into his living room. Waiting for him are four
men, standing: Virgil, Frankie (young wise-guy), Lenny (an old wise-
guy), and Tooth-pick Vic (a fireplug pitbull type).*

*Sitting in Cliff's recliner is Vincenzo Coccotti, the Frank Nitti to Detroit
mob leader Blue Lou Boyle.*

*Cliff is knocked to his knees. He looks up and sees the sitting Coccotti.
Dario and Lenny pick him up and roughly drop him in a chair.*

COCCOTTI
(*to Frankie*)
Tell Tooth-pick Vic to go outside and do you-know-what.

In Italian Frankie tells Tooth-pick Vic what Coccotti said. He nods and exits.

Cliff's chair is moved closer to Coccotti's. Dario stands on one side of Cliff. Frankie and Lenny ransack the trailer. Virgil has a bottle of Chivas Regal in his hand, but he has yet to touch a drop.

Do you know who I am, Mr Worley?

CLIFF
I give up. Who are you?

COCCOTTI
I'm the Anti-Christ. You get me in a vendetta kind of mood, you will tell the angels in Heaven that you had never seen pure evil so singularly personified as you did in the face of the man who killed you. My name is Vincenzo Coccotti. I work as counsel for Mr Blue Lou Boyle, the man your son stole from. I hear you were once a cop so I can assume you've heard of us before. Am I correct?

CLIFF
I've heard of Blue Lou Boyle.

COCCOTTI
I'm glad. Hopefully that will clear up the how-full-of-shit-I-am question you've been asking yourself. Now, we're gonna have a little Q and A, and, at the risk of sounding redundant, please make your answers genuine.
(*taking out a pack of Chesterfields*)
Want a Chesterfield?

CLIFF
No.

COCCOTTI
(*as he lights one up*)
I have a son of my own. About your boy's age. I can imagine how painful this must be for you. But Clarence and that bitch-whore girlfriend of his brought this all on themselves. And I implore you

29

not to go down that road with 'em. You can always take comfort in the fact that you never had a choice.

CLIFF

Look, I'd help ya if I could, but I haven't seen Clarence –

Before Cliff can finish his sentence, Coccotti slams him hard in the nose with his fist.

COCCOTTI

Smarts, don't it? Gettin' slammed in the nose fucks you all up. You got that pain shootin' through your brain. Your eyes fill up with water. It ain't any kind a fun. But what I have to offer you, that's as good as it's ever gonna get, and it won't ever get that good again. We talked to your neighbors, they saw a Mustang, a red Mustang, Clarence's red Mustang, parked in front of your trailer yesterday. Mr Worley, have you seen your son?

Cliff's defeated.

CLIFF

I've seen him.

COCCOTTI

Now I can't be sure of how much of what he told you. So in the chance you're in the dark about some of this, let me shed some light. That whore your boy hangs around with, her pimp is an associate of mine, and I don't just mean pimpin', in other affairs he works for me in a courier capacity. Well, apparently, that dirty little whore found out when we were gonna do some business, 'cause your son, the cowboy and his flame, came in the room blastin' and didn't stop till they were pretty sure everybody was dead.

CLIFF

What are you talkin' about?

COCCOTTI

I'm talkin' about a massacre. They snatched my narcotics and hightailed it outta there. Wouldda gotten away with it, but your son, fuckhead that he is, left his driver's license in a dead guy's hand. A whore hiding in the commode filled in all the blanks.

30

CLIFF

I don't believe you.

COCCOTTI

That's of minor importance. But what's of major fuckin'
importance is that I believe you. Where did they go?

CLIFF

On their honeymoon.

COCCOTTI

I'm gettin' angry askin' the same question a second time. Where
did they go?

CLIFF

They didn't tell me.

Coccotti looks at him.

Now, wait a minute and listen. I haven't seen Clarence in three
years. Yesterday he shows up here with a girl, sayin' he got
married. He told me he needed some quick cash for a honeymoon,
so he asked if he could borrow five hundred dollars. I wanted to
help him out so I wrote out a check. We went to breakfast and
that's the last I saw of him. So help me God.

They never thought to tell me where they were goin'. And I
never thought to ask.

*Coccotti looks at him for a long moment. He then gives Virgil a look.
Virgil, quick as greased lightning, grabs Cliff's hand and turns it palm
up. He then whips out a butterfly knife and slices Cliff's palm open and
pours Chivas Regal on the wound. Cliff screams.*

Coccotti puffs on a Chesterfield.

*Tooth-pick Vic returns to the trailer, and reports in Italian that there's
nothing in the car.*

*Virgil walks into the kitchen and gets a dishtowel. Cliff holds his bleeding
palm in agony. Virgil hands him the dishtowel. Cliff uses it to wrap up
his hand.*

COCCOTTI

Sicilians are great liars. The best in the world. I'm a Sicilian. And

31

my old man was the world heavyweight champion of Sicilian liars. And from growin' up with him I learned the pantomime. Now there are seventeen different things a guy can do when he lies to give him away. A guy has seventeen pantomimes. A woman's got twenty, but a guy's got seventeen. And if ya know 'em like ya know your own face, they beat lie detectors all to hell. What we got here is a little game of show and tell. You don't wanna show me nothing'. But you're tellin' me everything. Now I know you know where they are. So tell me, before I do some damage you won't walk away from.

The awful pain in Cliff's hand is being replaced by the awful pain in his heart. He looks deep into Coccotti's eyes.

                         CLIFF
Could I have one of those Chesterfields now?

                       COCCOTTI
Sure.

Coccotti leans over and hands him a smoke.

                         CLIFF
Got a match?

Cliff reaches into his pocket and pulls out a lighter.

Oh, don't bother. I got one.
                    (*he lights the cigarette*)
So you're a Sicilian, huh?

                       COCCOTTI
                      (*intensely*)
Uh-huh.

                         CLIFF
You know I read a lot. Especially things that have to do with history. I find that shit fascinating. In fact, I don't know if you know this or not, Sicilians were spawned by niggers.

All the men stop what they are doing and look at Cliff, except for Tooth-pick Vic, who doesn't speak English and so isn't insulted. Coccotti can't believe what he's hearing.

32

COCCOTTI

Come again?

CLIFF

It's a fact. Sicilians have nigger blood pumpin' through their
hearts. If you don't believe me, look it up. You see, hundreds and
hundreds of years ago the Moors conquered Sicily. And Moors are
niggers. Way back then, Sicilians were like the wops in northern
Italy. Blond hair, blue eyes. But, once the Moors moved in there,
they changed the whole country. They did so much fuckin' with
the Sicilian women, they changed the blood-line for ever, from
blond hair and blue eyes to black hair and dark skin. I find it
absolutely amazing to think that to this day, hundreds of years
later, Sicilians still carry that nigger gene. I'm just quotin' history.
It's a fact. It's written. Your ancestors were niggers. Your great,
great, great, great, great-grandmother was fucked by a nigger, and
had a half-nigger kid. That is a fact. Now tell me, am I lyin'?

*Coccotti looks at him for a moment then jumps up, whips out an
automatic, grabs hold of Cliff's hair, puts the barrel to his temple, and
pumps three bullets through Cliff's head.*

*He pushes the body violently aside. Coccotti pauses. Unable to express his
feelings and frustrated by the blood on his hands, he simply drops his
weapon, and turns to his men.*

COCCOTTI

I haven't killed anybody since 1974. Goddamn his soul to burn for
eternity in fuckin' hell for makin' me spill blood on my hands! Go
to this comedian's son's apartment and come back with somethin'
that tells me where that asshole went so I can wipe this egg off of
my face and fix this fucked-up family for good.

*Tooth-pick Vic taps Frankie's shoulder and, in Italian, asks him what
that was all about.*

*Lenny, who has been going through Cliff's refrigerator, has found a beer.
When he closes the refrigerator door he finds a note held on by a ceramic
banana magnet that says: 'Clarence in LA: Dick Ritchie (Number and
address)'.*

LENNY

Boss, get ready to get happy.

TITLE CARD:

'CLARENCE AND ALABAMA HIT LA'

INT. DICK'S APARTMENT – MORNING

Dick's asleep in a recliner. He's wearing his clothes from the night before. His room-mate Floyd is lying on the sofa watching TV.

The sound of four hands knocking on his door wakes Dick up. He shakes the bats out of his belfry, opens the door, and finds the cutest couple in Los Angeles standing in his doorway.

Clarence and Alabama immediately start singing 'Hello My Baby' like the frog in the old Chuck Jones cartoon.

CLARENCE/ALABAMA

Hello my baby,
Hello my honey,
Hello my ragtime gal –

DICK

Hi, guys.

Alabama throws her arms around Dick, and gives him a quick kiss. After she breaks, Clarence does the same. Clarence and Alabama walk right past Dick and into his apartment.

CLARENCE

Wow. Neat place.

INT. PINK'S HOT-DOG STAND – DAY

The Pink's employees work like skilled Benihana chefs as they assemble the ultimate masterpiece hot-dog.

EXT. PINK'S HOT-DOG STAND – PATIO – DAY

Clarence, Alabama, and Dick are sitting at an outdoor table chowing down on chili dogs. Alabama is in the middle of a story.

ALABAMA

. . . when my mom went into labor, my dad panicked. He never had a kid before, and crashed the car. Now, picture this: their car's demolished, crowd is starting to gather, my mom is yelling, going into contractions, and my dad, who was losing it before, is now completely screaming yellow zonkers. Then, out of nowhere, as if from thin air, this big giant bus appears, and the bus-driver says, 'Get her in here.' He forgot all about his route and just drove straight to the hospital. So, because he was such a nice guy, they wanted to name the baby after him, as a sign of gratitude. Well, his name was Waldo, and no matter how grateful they were, even if I'da been a boy, they wouldn't call me Waldo. So, they asked Waldo where he was from. And, so there you go.

CLARENCE

And here we are.

DICK

That's a pretty amazing story.

CLARENCE

Well, she's a pretty amazing girl. What are women like out here?

DICK

Just like in Detroit, only skinnier.

CLARENCE

You goin' out?

DICK

Well, for the past couple of years I've been goin' out with girls from my acting class.

CLARENCE

Good for you.

DICK

What's so fuckin' good about it? Actresses are the most fucked-in-the-head bunch of women in the world. It's like they gotta pass a test of emotional instability before they can get their SAG card. Oh, guess what? I had a really good reading for *T. J. Hooker* the other day.

ALABAMA

You're gonna be on *T. J. Hooker*?

DICK

Knock wood.

He knocks the table and then looks at it.

. . . formica. I did real well. I think she liked me.

CLARENCE

Did you meet Captain Kirk?

DICK

You don't meet him in the audition. That comes later. Hope, hope.

ALABAMA
(finishing her hot-dog)

That was so good I'm gonna have another.

DICK

You can't have just one.

Alabama leaves to get another hot-dog. Clarence never takes his eyes off her.

How much of that letter was on the up and up?

CLARENCE

Every word of it.

Dick sees where Clarence's attention is.

DICK

You're really in love, aren't you?

CLARENCE

For the very first time in my life.
(pause)
Do you know what that's like?

Clarence is so intense Dick doesn't know how to answer.

                        DICK
                    (*regretfully*)
No I don't.
                (*he looks at Alabama*)
How did you two meet?

Clarence leans back thoughtfully and takes a sip from his Hebrew cream soda.

                      CLARENCE
Do you remember The Lyric?

INT. THE LYRIC THEATER – NIGHT

Sonny Chiba, as 'Streetfighter' Terry Surki, drives into a group of guys, fists and feet flying and whips ass on the silver screen.

Clarence sits, legs over the back of the chair in front of him, nibbling on popcorn, eyes big as saucers, and a big smile on his face.

EXT. THE LYRIC THEATER – NIGHT

A cab pulls up to the outside of The Lyric. The marquee carries the names of the triple feature: The Streetfighter, Return of the Streetfighter, *and* Sister Streetfighter. *Alabama steps out of the taxi cab and walks up to the box office.*

A box office girl reading comic looks at her.

                      ALABAMA
One please.

                  BOX OFFICE GIRL
Ninety-nine cents.

                      ALABAMA
Which one is on now?

                  BOX OFFICE GIRL
Return of the Streetfighter. It's been on about forty-five minutes.

INT. THE LYRIC THEATER — LOBBY — NIGHT

Alabama walks into the lobby and goes over to the concession stand. A young usher takes care of her.

> ALABAMA
> Can I have a medium popcorn? A super-large Mr Pibb, and a box of Goobers.

INT. THE LYRIC THEATER — NIGHT

It's still assholes and elbows on the screen with Sonny Chiba taking on all-comers.

Alabama walks through the doors with her bounty of food. She makes a quick scan of the theater. Not many people are there. She makes a beeline for the front which so happens to be Clarence's area of choice. She picks the row of seats just behind Clarence and starts asking her way down it.

Clarence turns and sees this beautiful girl all alone moving towards him. He turns his attention back to the screen, trying not to be so obvious.

When Alabama gets right behind Clarence, her foot thunks a discarded wine bottle, causing her to trip and spill her popcorn over Clarence.

> ALABAMA
> Oh, look what happened. Oh God, I'm so sorry. Are you OK?

> CLARENCE
> Yeah. I'm fine. It didn't hurt.

> ALABAMA
> I'm the clumsiest person in the world.

> CLARENCE
> *(picking popcorn out of his hair)*
> It's OK. Don't worry about it. Accidents happen.

> ALABAMA
> *(picking popcorn out of his hair)*
> What a wonderful philosophy. Thanks for being such a sweetheart. You could have been a real dick.

Alabama sits back in her seat to watch the movie.

Clarence tries to wipe her out of his mind, which isn't easy, and get back into the movie.

They both watch the screen for a moment. Then, Alabama leans forward and taps Clarence on the shoulder.

Excuse me . . . I hate to bother you again. Would you mind too terribly filling me in on what I missed?

Jumping at this opportunity.

> CLARENCE
> Not at all. OK, this guy here, he's Sonny Chiba.

> ALABAMA
> The oriental.

> CLARENCE
> The oriental in black. He's an assassin. Now, at the beginning he was hired to kill this guy the cops had. So he got himself arrested. They take him into the police station. And he starts kickin' all the cops' asses. Now, while keepin' them at bay, he finds the guy he was supposed to kill. Does a number on him. Kicks the cops' asses some more. Kicks the bars out of the window. And jumps out into a getaway car that was waiting for him.

> ALABAMA
> Want some Goobers?

> CLARENCE
> Thanks a lot.

> ALABAMA
> I thought Sonny was the good guy.

> CLARENCE
> He ain't so much good guy as he's just a bad motherfucker. Sonny don't be bullshittin'. He fucks dudes up for life. Hold on, a fight scene's comin' up.

They both watch, eyes wide, as Sonny Chiba kicks ass.

TIMECUT:

On the screen, Sonny Chiba's all jacked up. Dead bodies lie all around him. THE END (in Japanese) flashes on the screen.

The theater lights go up. Alabama's now sitting in the seat next to Clarence. They're both applauding.

ALABAMA

Great movie. Action-packed!

CLARENCE

Does Sonny kick ass or does Sonny kick ass?

ALABAMA

Sonny kicks ass.

CLARENCE

You shouldda saw the first original uncut version of the *Streetfighter*. It was the only movie up to that time rated X for violence. But we just saw the R.

ALABAMA

If that was the R, I'd love to see the X.

CLARENCE

My name is Clarence, and what is yours?

ALABAMA

Alabama Whitman. Pleased to meet ya.

CLARENCE

Is that your real name? Really?

ALABAMA

That's my real name, really. I got proof. See.

She shows Clarence her driver's license.

CLARENCE

Well, cut my legs off and call me Shorty. That's a pretty original moniker there, Alabama. Sounds like a Pam Grier movie.
(*announcer voice*)
She's a sixteen-calibre kitten, equally equipped for killin' an lovin'! She carried a sawed-off shotgun in her purse, a black belt around her waist, and the white-hot fire of hate in her eyes! Alabama Whitman is Pam Grier! Pray for forgiveness. Rated R . . . for Ruthless Revenge!

Clarence and Alabama are outside the theater. With the marquee lit up in the background they both perform unskilled martial arts moves. Clarence and Alabama break up laughing.

> CLARENCE

Where's your car? I'll walk you to it.

> ALABAMA

I took a cab.

> CLARENCE

You took a cab to see three kung fu movies?

> ALABAMA

Sure. Why not?

> CLARENCE

Nothing. It's just you're a girl after my own heart.

> ALABAMA

What time is it?

> CLARENCE

'Bout twelve.

> ALABAMA

I suppose you gotta get up early, huh?

> CLARENCE

No. Not particularly.

> *(pause)*

How come?

> ALABAMA

Well, it's just when I see a really good movie I really like to go out and get some pie, and talk about it. It's sort of a tradition. Do you like to eat pie after you've seen a good movie?

> CLARENCE

I love to get pie after a movie.

> ALABAMA

Would you like to get some pie?

41

CLARENCE

I'd love some pie.

INT. DENNY'S RESTAURANT — NIGHT

Clarence and Alabama are sitting in a booth at an all-night Denny's. It's about 12:30 a.m. Clarence is having a piece of chocolate cream pie and a Coke. Alabama's nibbling on a piece of heated apple pie and sipping on a large Tab.

CLARENCE

Well, enough about the King. How about you?

ALABAMA

How 'bout me what?

CLARENCE

Tell me about yourself.

ALABAMA

There's nothing to tell.

CLARENCE

C'mon. What're ya tryin' to be? The Phantom Lady?

ALABAMA

What do you want to know?

CLARENCE

Well, for starters, what do you do? Where're ya from? What's your favorite color? Who's your favorite movie star? What kinda music do you like? What are your turn-ons and turn-offs? Do you have a fella? What's the story behind you takin' a cab to the most dangerous part of town alone? And, in a theater full of empty seats, why did you sit by me?

Alabama takes a bite of pie, puts down her fork, and looks at Clarence.

ALABAMA

Ask me them again. One by one.

CLARENCE

What do you do?

ALABAMA

I don't remember.

CLARENCE

Where are you from?

ALABAMA

I might be from Tallahassee. But I'm not sure yet.

CLARENCE

What's your favorite color?

ALABAMA

I don't remember. But off the top of my head, I'd say black.

CLARENCE

Who's your favorite movie star?

ALABAMA

Burt Reynolds.

CLARENCE

Would you like a bite of my pie?

ALABAMA

Yes, I would.

Clarence scoops up a piece on his fork and Alabama bites it off.

CLARENCE

Like it?

ALABAMA

Very much. Now, where were we?

CLARENCE

What kinda music do you like?

ALABAMA

Phil Spector. Girl group stuff. You know, like 'He's a Rebel.'

CLARENCE

What are your turn-ons?

ALABAMA

Mickey Rourke, somebody who can appreciate the finer things in

43

life, like Elvis's voice, good kung fu, and a tasty piece of pie.

CLARENCE

Turn-offs?

ALABAMA

I'm sure there must be something, but I don't really remember.
The only thing that comes to mind are Persians.

CLARENCE

Do you have a fella?

She looks at Clarence and smiles.

ALABAMA

I'm not sure yet. Ask me again later.

CLARENCE

What's the story behind you takin' a cab to the most dangerous
part of town alone?

ALABAMA

Apparently, I was hit on the head with something really heavy,
giving me a form of amnesia. When I came to, I didn't know who I
was, where I was, or where I came from. Luckily, I had my
driver's license or I wouldn't even know my name. I hoped it
would tell me where I lived but it had a Tallahassee address on it,
and I stopped somebody on the street and they told me I was in
Detroit. So that was no help. But I did have some money on me,
so I hopped in a cab until I saw somethin' that looked familiar.
For some reason, and don't ask me why, that theater looked
familiar. So I told him to stop and I got out.

CLARENCE

And in a theater full of empty seats, why did you sit by me?

ALABAMA

Because you looked like a nice guy, and I was a little scared. And I
sure couldda used a nice guy about that time, so I spilled my
popcorn on you.

*Clarence looks at her closely. He picks up his soda and sucks on the straw
until it makes that slurping sound. He puts it aside and stares into her
soul.*

A smile cracks on her face and develops into a big wide grin.

Aren't you just dazzled by my imagination, lover boy?
                    (*eats her last piece of pie*)
Where to next?

INT. COMIC BOOK STORE – NIGHT

It's about 1:30 a.m. Clarence has taken Alabama to where he works. It's a comic book store called Heroes For Sale. Alabama thinks this place is super-cool.

                    ALABAMA
Wow. What a swell place to work.

                    CLARENCE
Yeah, I got the key, so I come here at night, hang out, read comic books, play music.

                    ALABAMA
How long have you worked here?

                    CLARENCE
Almost four years.

                    ALABAMA
That's a long time.

                    CLARENCE
I'm hip. But you know, I'm comfortable here. It's easy work. I know what I'm doing. Everybody who works here is my buddy. I'm friendly with most of the customers. I just hang around and talk about comic books all day.

                    ALABAMA
Do you get paid a lot?

                    CLARENCE
That's where trouble comes into paradise. But the boss let's you borrow money if you need it. Wanna see what *Spiderman* number one looks like?

                    ALABAMA
You bet. How much is that worth?

45

Clarence gets a box off the shelf.

CLARENCE
Four hundred bucks.

ALABAMA
I didn't even know they had stores that just sold comic books.

CLARENCE
Well, we sell other things too. Cool stuff. *Man from U.N.C.L.E.*
lunch boxes. *Green Hornet* board games. Shit like that. But comic
books are our main business. There's a lot of collectors around here.

She holds up a little GI Joe sized action figure of a black policeman.

ALABAMA
What's that?

CLARENCE
That's a *Rookies* doll. George Sanford Brown. We gotta lotta dolls.
They're real cool. Did you know they came out with dolls for all
the actors in *The Black Hole*? I always found it funny that
somewhere there's a kid playin' with a little figure of Ernest
Borgnine.

He pulls out a plastic-encased Spiderman *comic from the box.*

Spiderman, number one. The one that started it all.

Clarence shows the comic book to Alabama.

ALABAMA
God, Spiderman looks different.

CLARENCE
He was just born, remember? This is the first one. You know that
guy, Dr Gene Scott? He said that the story of Spiderman is the
story of Christ, just disguised. Well, I thought about that even
before I heard him say it. Hold on, let me show you my favorite
comic book cover of all time.

He pulls out another comic

Sgt Fury and His Howling Commandos. One of the coolest series
known to man. They're completely worthless. You can get

46

number one for about four bucks. But that's one of the cool things about them, they're so cheap.

(*he opens one up*)

Just look at that artwork, will ya. Great stories. Great characters. Look at this one.

We see the Sgt Fury *panels.*

Nick's gotten a ring for his sweetheart and he wears it around his neck on a chain. OK, later in the story he gets into a fight with a Nazi bastard on a ship. He knocks the guy overboard, but the Kraut grabs ahold of his chain and the ring goes overboard too. So, Nick dives into the ocean to get it. Isn't that cool?

She's looking into Clarence's eyes. He turns and meets her gaze.

Alabama, I'd like you to have this.

Clarence hands her the Sgt Fury and His Howling Commandos *comic book that he loves so much.*

INT. CLARENCE'S APARTMENT — BEDROOM — NIGHT

Clarence's bedroom is a pop culture explosion. Movie posters, pictures of Elvis, anything you can imagine. The two walk through the door.

ALABAMA

What a cool room!

She runs and does a jumping somersault into his bed.

Later. Alabama's sitting Indian-style going through Clarence's photo album. Clarence is behind her planting little kisses on her neck and shoulders.

Oooooh, you look so cute in your little cowboy outfit. How old were you then?

CLARENCE

Five.

She turns the page.

ALABAMA

Oh, you looked so cute as a little Elvis.

CLARENCE

I finally knew what I wanted to be when I grew up.

LATER – LIVING ROOM

Clarence and Alabama slow dance in the middle of his room to Janis Joplin's 'Piece of My Heart.'

CLARENCE

You know when you sat behind me?

ALABAMA

At the movies?

CLARENCE

Uh-huh, I was tryin' to think of somethin' to say to you, then I thought, she doesn't want me bothering her.

ALABAMA

What would make you think that?

CLARENCE

I dunno. I guess I'm just stupid.

ALABAMA

You're not stupid. Just wrong.

They move to the music. Alabama softly, quietly sings some of the words to the song.

I love Janis.

CLARENCE

You know, a lot of people have misconceptions of how she died.

ALABAMA

She OD'd, didn't she?

CLARENCE

Yeah, she OD'd. But she wasn't on her last legs or anythin'. She didn't take too much. It shouldn't have killed her. There was somethin' wrong with what she took.

ALABAMA

You mean she got a bad batch?

CLARENCE

That's what happened. In fact, when she died, it was considered
to be the happiest time of her life. She'd been fucked over so much
by men she didn't trust them. She was havin' this relationship
with this guy and he asked her to marry him. Now, other people
had asked to marry her before, but she couldn't be sure whether
they really loved her or were just after her money. So, she said no.
And the guy says, 'Look, I really love you, and I wanna prove it.
So have your lawyers draw up a paper that says no matter what
happens, I can never get any of your money, and I'll sign it.' So
she did, and he did, and he asked her, and she said yes. And once
they were engaged he told her a secret about himself that she never
knew; he was a millionaire.

ALABAMA

So he really loved her?

CLARENCE

Uh-huh.

They kiss.

INT. CLARENCE'S APARTMENT – BEDROOM – DAY

*It's the next day, around 1 p.m. Clarence wakes up in his bed, alone. He
looks around, and no Alabama. Then he hears crying in the distance. He
puts on a robe and investigates.*

INT. CLARENCE'S APARTMENT – LIVING ROOM – DAY

*Alabama's wearing one of Clarence's old shirts. She's curled up in a chair
crying. Clarence approaches her. She tries to compose herself.*

CLARENCE

What's wrong, sweetheart? Did I do something? What did I do?

ALABAMA

You didn't do nothing.

CLARENCE

Did you hurt yourself?

(he takes her foot)
Whatd'ya do? Step on a thumbtack?

ALABAMA

Clarence, I've got something to tell you. I didn't just happen to be at that theater. I was paid to be there.

CLARENCE

What are you, a theater checker? You check up on the box office girls. Make sure they're not rippin' the place off.

ALABAMA

I'm not a theater checker. I'm a call girl.

Pause.

CLARENCE

You're a whore?

ALABAMA

I'm a call girl. There's a difference, ya know.
(pause)
I don't know. Maybe there's not. That place you took me to last night, that comic book place.

CLARENCE

Heroes For Sale?

ALABAMA

Yeah, that one. Somebody who works there arranged to have me meet you.

CLARENCE

Who?

ALABAMA

I don't know, I didn't talk with them. The plan was for me to bump into you, pick you up, spend the night, and skip out after you fell asleep. I was gonna write you a note and say that this was my last day in America. That I was leaving on a plane this morning to the Ukraine to marry a rich millionaire, and thank you for making my last day in America my best day.

CLARENCE

That dazzling imagination.

ALABAMA

It's over on the TV. All it says is: Dear Clarence. I couldn't write anymore. I didn't not want to ever see you again. In fact, it's stupid not to ever see you again. Last night . . . I don't know . . . I felt . . . I hadn't had that much fun since Girl Scouts. So I just said, 'Alabama, come clean. Let him know what's what, and if he tells you to go fuck yourself then go back to Drexl and fuck yourself.'

CLARENCE

Who and what is a Drexl?

ALABAMA

My pimp.

CLARENCE

You have a pimp?

ALABAMA

Uh-huh.

CLARENCE

A real live pimp?

ALABAMA

Uh-huh.

CLARENCE

Is he black?

ALABAMA

He thinks he is. He says his mother was Apache, but I suspect he's lying.

CLARENCE

Is he nice?

ALABAMA

Well, I wouldn't go so far as to call him nice, but he's treated me pretty decent. But I've only been there about four days. He got a little rough with Arlene the other day.

CLARENCE

What did he do to Arlene?

ALABAMA

Slapped her around a little. Punched her in the stomach. It was pretty scary.

CLARENCE

This motherfucker sounds charming!

Clarence is on his feet, furious.

Goddamn it, Alabama, you gotta get the fuck outta there! How much longer before he's slappin' you around? Punchin' you in the stomach? How the fuck did you get hooked up with a douche-bag like this in the first place?

ALABAMA

As the bus station. He said I'd be a perfect call girl. And that he knew an agency in California that, on his recommendation, would handle me. They have a very exclusive clientele: movie stars, big businessmen, total white-collar. And all the girls in the agency get a grand a night. At least five hundred. They drive Porsches, live in condos, have stockbrokers, carry beepers, you know, like Nancy Allen in *Dressed to Kill*. And when I was ready he'd call 'em, give me a plane ticket, and send me on my way. He says he makes a nice finder's fee for finding them hot prospects. But no one's gonna pay a grand a night for a girl who doesn't know whether to shit or wind her watch. So what I'm doin' for Drexl now is just sorta learnin' the ropes. It seemed like a lotta fun, but I don't really like it much, till last night. You were only my third trick, but you didn't feel like a trick. Since it was a secret, I just pretended I was on a date. And, um, I guess I want a second date.

CLARENCE

Thank you. I wanna see you again too. And again, and again, and again. Bama, I know we haven't known each other long, but my parents went together all throughout high school, and they still got a divorce. So, fuck it, you wanna marry me?

ALABAMA

What?

CLARENCE

Will you be my wife?

When Alabama gives her answer, her voice cracks.

ALABAMA

Yes.

CLARENCE
(*a little surprised*)

You will?

ALABAMA

You better not be fucking teasing me.

CLARENCE

You better not be fuckin' teasin' me.

They seal it with a kiss.

LATER — THAT NIGHT

CU – Alabama's wedding ring.

The newlyweds are snuggling up together on the couch watching TV. The movie they're watching is The Incredible One-Armed Boxer vs. the Master of the Flying Guillotine. *Alabama watches the screen, but every so often she looks down to admire the ring on her hand.*

CLARENCE

Did ya ever see *The Chinese Professionals*?

ALABAMA

I don't believe so.

CLARENCE

Well, that's the one that explains how Jimmy Wang Yu became the Incredible One-Armed Boxer.

We hear, off screen, the TV Announcer say:

TV ANNOUNCER
(*off*)

We'll return to Jimmy Wang Yu in . . . *The Incredible One-Armed Boxer vs. the Master of the Flying Guillotine*, tonight's eight o'clock

53

movie, after these important messages . . .

Clarence looks at the TV. He feels the warmth of Alabama's hand holding his. We see commercials playing.

He turns in her direction. She's absent-mindedly looking at her wedding ring.

He smiles and turns back to the TV.

More commercials.

Dolly close on Clarence's face.

FLASH ON:

Alabama, right after he proposed.

ALABAMA
You better not be fucking teasing me.

FLASH ON:

In a cute, all-night wedding chapel. Clarence dressed in a rented tuxedo and Alabama in a rented white wedding gown.

ALABAMA
I do.

CLARENCE
Thank you.

FLASH ON:

Clarence and Alabama, dressed in tux and gown, doing a lovers' waltz on a ballroom dance floor.

FLASH ON:

Clarence and Alabama in a taxi cab.

CLARENCE
Hello, Mrs Worley.

ALABAMA
How do you do, Mr Worley?

CLARENCE
Top o' the morning to you, Mrs Worley.

54

ALABAMA

Bottom of the ninth. Mr Worley. Oh, by the by, Mr Worley, have you seen your lovely wife today?

CLARENCE

Oh, you're speaking of my charming wife Mrs Alabama Worley.

ALABAMA

Of course. Are there others, Mr Worley?

Moving on top of her.

CLARENCE

Not for me.

He starts kissing her and moving her down on the seat. She resists.

ALABAMA
(*playfully*)

No no no no no no no no no . . .

CLARENCE
(*playfully*)

Yes yes yes yes yes yes yes yes . . .

FLASH ON:

A big mean-looking black man in pimp's clothes.

PIMP

Bitch, you better git yo ass back on the street an' git me my money!

FLASH ON:

Pimp on street corner with his arm around Alabama, giving a sales pitch to a potential customer.

PIMP

I'm tellin' you, my man, this bitch is fine. This girl's a freak! You can fuck 'er in the ass, fuck 'er in the mouth. Rough stuff, too. She's a freak for it. Jus' try not to fuck 'er up for life.

FLASH ON:

Pimp beating Alabama.

You holdin' out on me, girl? Bitch, you never learn!

FLASH ON:

Alabama passionately kissing the uninterested pimp.

PIMP

Hang it up, momma. I got no time for this bullshit.

BACK TO:

TV showing kung fu film.

Back to Clarence's face. There's definitely something different about his eyes.

Clarence springs off the couch and goes into his bedroom. Alabama's startled by his sudden movement.

ALABAMA
(*yelling after him*)

Where you goin', honey?

CLARENCE
(*off*)

I just gotta get somethin'.

INT. CLARENCE'S APARTMENT – BATHROOM – NIGHT

Clarence splashes water on his face, trying to wash away the images that keep polluting his mind. Then, he hears a familiar voice.

FAMILIAR VOICE
(*off*)

Well? Can you live with it?

Clarence turns and sees that the voice belongs to Elvis Presley. Clarence isn't surprised to see him.

CLARENCE

What?

ELVIS

Can you live with it?

CLARENCE

Live with what?

ELVIS

With that son of a bitch walkin' around breathin' the same air as you? And gettin' away with it every day. Are you haunted?

CLARENCE

Yeah.

ELVIS

You wanna get unhaunted?

CLARENCE

Yeah.

ELVIS

Then shoot 'em. Shoot 'em in the face. And feed that boy to the dogs.

CLARENCE

I can't believe what the fuck you're tellin' me.

ELVIS

I ain't tellin' ya nothin'. I'm just sayin' what I'd do.

CLARENCE

You'd really do that?

ELVIS

He don't got no right to live.

CLARENCE

Look, Elvis, he is hauntin' me. He doesn't deserve to live. And I do want to kill him. But I don't wanna go to jail for the rest of my life.

ELVIS

I don't blame you.

CLARENCE

If I thought I could get away with it –

ELVIS

Killin' 'em's the hard part. Gettin' away with it's the easy part. Whaddya think the cops do when a pimp's killed? Burn the midnight oil tryin' to find who done it? They couldn't give a flyin'

57

fuck if all the pimps in the whole wide world took two in the back of the fuckin' head. If you don't get caught at the scene with the smokin' gun in your hand, you got away with it.

Clarence looks at Elvis.

Clarence, I like ya. Always have, always will.

INT. CLARENCE'S APARTMENT – BEDROOM – NIGHT

CU – A snub-nosed .38, which Clarence loads and sticks down his heavy athletic sock.

INT. CLARENCE'S APARTMENT – LIVING ROOM – NIGHT

Clarence returns.

> CLARENCE
> Sweetheart, write down your former address.

> ALABAMA
> What?

> CLARENCE
> Write down Drexl's address.

> ALABAMA
> Why?

> CLARENCE
> So I can go over there and pick up your things.

> ALABAMA
> *(really scared)*
> No, Clarence. Just forget it, babe. I just wanna disappear from there.

He kneels down before her and holds her hand.

> CLARENCE
> Look, sweetheart, he scares you. But I'm not scared of that motherfucker. He can't touch you now. You're completely out of his reach. He poses absolutely no threat to us. So, if he doesn't matter, which he doesn't, it would be stupid to lose your things, now wouldn't it.

ALABAMA

You don't know him –

CLARENCE

You don't know me. Not when it comes to shit like this. I have to do this. I need for you to know you can count on me to protect you. Now write down the address.

TITLE CARD:

'CASS QUARTER, HEART OF DETROIT'

EXT. DOWNTOWN DETROIT STREET – NIGHT

It's pretty late at night. Clarence steps out of his red Mustang. He's right smack dab in the middle of a bad place to be in the daytime. He checks the pulse on his neck; it's beating like a race horse. To pump himself up he does a quick Elvis Presley gyration.

CLARENCE
(*in Elvis voice*)

Yeah . . . yeah . . .

He makes a beeline for the front door of a large, dark apartment building.

INT. DARK BUILDING – NIGHT

He's inside. His heart's really racing now. He has the TV guide that Alabama wrote the address on in his hand. He climbs a flight of stairs and makes his way down a dark hallway to apartment 22, the residence of Drexl Spivey. Clarence knocks on the door.

A Young Black Man, about twenty years old, answers the door. He has really big biceps and is wearing a black and white fishnet football jersey.

YOUNG BLACK MAN

You want somethin'?

CLARENCE

Drexl?

59

YOUNG BLACK MAN
Naw, man, I'm Marty. Whatcha want?

CLARENCE
I gotta talk to Drexl.

MARTY
Well, what the fuck you wanna tell him?

CLARENCE
It's about Alabama.

A figure jumps in the doorway wearing a yellow Farah Fawcett T-shirt. It's our friend, Drexl Spivey.

DREXL
Where the fuck is that bitch?

CLARENCE
She's with me.

DREXL
Who the fuck are you?

CLARENCE
I'm her husband.

DREXL
Well. That makes us practically related. Bring your ass on in.

INT. DREXL'S LIVING ROOM – NIGHT

Drexl and Marty about-face and walk into the room, continuing a conversation they were having and leaving Clarence standing in the doorway. This is not the confrontation Clarence expected. He trails in behind Drexl and Marty.

DREXL
(*to Marty*)
What was I sayin'?

MARTY
Rock whores.

60

DREXL

You ain't seen nothin' like these rock whores. They ass be young man. They got that fine young pussy. Bitches want the rock they be a freak for you. They give you hips, lips, and fingertips.

Drexl looks over his shoulder at Clarence.

(*to Clarence*)
You know what I'm talkin' about.

Drexl gestures to one of the three stoned Hookers lounging about the apartment.

(*to Marty*)
These bitches over here ain't shit. You stomp them bitches to death to get to the kind of pussy I'm talkin' about.

Drexl sits down at a couch with a card table in front of it, scattered with take-out boxes of Chinese food. A black exploitation movie is playing on TV.

Looky here, you want the bitches to really fly high, make your rocks with Cherry Seven-Up.

MARTY

Pussy love pink rocks.

This is not how Clarence expected to confront Drexl, but this is exactly what he expected Drexl to be like. He positions himself in front of the food table, demanding Drexl's attention.

DREXL
(*eating with chopsticks, to Clarence*)
Grab a seat there, boy. Want some dinner? Grab yourself an egg roll. We got everything here from a diddle-eyed-Joe to a damned-if-I-know.

CLARENCE

No thanks.

DREXL

No thanks? What does that mean? Means you ate before you came on down here? All full. Is that it? Naw, I don't think so. I think you're too scared to be eatin'. Now, see we're sittin' down here, ready to negotiate, and you've already given up your shit. I'm still a mystery to you. But I know exactly where your ass is comin' from.

See, if I asked you if you wanted some dinner and you grabbed an egg roll and started to chow down, I'd say to myself, 'This motherfucker's carryin' on like he ain't got a care in the world. Who knows? Maybe he don't. Maybe this fool's such a bad motherfucker, he don't got to worry about nothin', he just sit down, eat my Chinese, watch my TV.' See? You ain't even sat down yet. On that TV there, since you been in the room, is a woman with her titties hangin' out, and you ain't even bothered to look. You just been starin' at me. Now, I know I'm pretty, but I ain't as pretty as a couple of titties.

Clarence takes out an envelope and throws it on the table.

CLARENCE
I'm not eatin' cause I'm not hungry. I'm not sittin' 'cause I'm not stayin'. I'm not lookin' at the movie 'cause I saw it seven years ago. It's *The Mack* with Max Julian, Carol Speed, and Richard Pryor, written by Bobby Poole, directed by Michael Campus, and released by Cinerama Releasing Company in 1984. I'm not scared of you. I just don't like you. In that envelope is some payoff money. Alabama's moving on to some greener pastures. We're not negotiatin'. I don't like to barter. I don't like to dicker. I never have fun in Tijuana. That price is non-negotiable. What's in that envelope is for my peace of mind. My peace of mind is worth that much. Not one penny more, not one penny more.

You could hear a pin drop. Once Clarence starts talking Marty goes on full alert. Drexl stops eating and the Whores stop breathing. All eyes are on Drexl. Drexl drops his chopsticks and opens the envelope. It's empty.

DREXL
It's empty.

Clarence flashes a wide Cheshire cat grin that says, 'That's right, asshole.'

Silence.

Ooooooooooh weeeeeeee! This child is terrible. Marty, you know what we got here? Motherfuckin' Charles Bronson. Is that who you supposed to be? Mr Majestyk? Looky here, Charlie, none of this shit is necessary. I ain't got no hold on Alabama. I just tryin' to lend the girl a helpin' hand –

Before Drexl finishes his sentence he picks up the card table and throws it at Clarence, catching him off guard.

Marty comes up behind Clarence and throws his arm around his neck, putting him in a tight choke hold.

Clarence, with his free arm, hits Marty hard with his elbow in the solar plexus. We'll never know if that blow had any effect because at just that moment Drexl takes a flying leap and tackles the two guys.

All of them go crashing into the stereo unit and a couple of shelves that hold records, all of which collapse to the floor in a shower of LPs.

Marty, who's on the bottom of the pile, hasn't let go of Clarence.

Since Drexl's on top, he starts slamming his fists into Clarence's face.

Clarence, who's sandwiched between these two guys, can't do a whole lot about it.

Ya wanna fuck wit me?
                    (*hits Clarence*)
Ya wanna fuck wit me?
                    (*hits Clarence*)
I'll show ya who you're fuckin' wit!

He hits Clarence hard in the face with both fists.

Clarence, who has no leverage whatsoever, grabs hold of Drexl's face and digs his nails in. He sticks his thumb in Drexl's mouth, grabs a piece of cheek, and starts twisting.

Marty, who's in an even worse position, can do nothing but tighten his grip around Clarence's neck, until Clarence feels like his eyes are going to pop out of his head.

Drexl's face is getting torn up, but he's also biting down hard on Clarence's thumb.

Clarence raises his head and brings it down fast, crunching Marty's face, and busting his nose.

Marty loosens his grip around Clarence's neck. Clarence wiggles free and gets up on to his knees.

Drexl and Clarence are now on an even but awkward footing. The two are going at each other like a pair of alley cats, not aiming their punches, just keeping them coming fast and furious. They're not doing much damage to each other because of their positions, it's almost like a hockey fight.

Marty sneaks up behind Clarence and smashes him in the head with a stack of LPs. This disorients Clarence. Marty grabs him from behind and pulls him to his feet.

Drexl socks him in the face: one, two, three! Then he kicks him hard in the balls.

Marty lets go and Clarence hits the ground like a sack of potatoes. He curls up into a fetal position and holds his balls, tears coming out of his eyes.

Drexl's face is torn up from Clarence's nails.

Marty has blood streaming down his face from his nose and on to his shirt.

(*to Marty*)
You OK? That stupid dumb-ass didn't break your nose, did he?

MARTY
Naw. It don't feel too good but it's all right.

Drexl kicks Clarence, who's still on the ground hurting.

DREXL
(*to Clarence*)
You see what you get when you fuck wit me, white boy? You're gonna walk in my goddamn house, my house! Gonna come in here and tell me! Talkin' that smack, in my house, in front of my employees. Shit! Your ass must be crazy.
(*to Marty*)
I don't think this white boy's got good sense. Hey, Marty.

(*laughing*)
He must of thought it was white boy day. It ain't white boy day, is it?

                    MARTY
                  (*laughing*)
Naw, man, it ain't white boy day.

                    DREXL
                  (*to Clarence*)
Shit, man, you done fucked up again. Next time you bogart your way into a nigger's crib, an' get all in his face, make sure you do it on white boy day.

                    CLARENCE
                  (*hurting*)
Wannabee nigger . . .

                    DREXL
Fuck you! My mother was Apache.

Drexl kicks him again. Clarence curls up.

Drexl bends down and looks for Clarence's wallet in his jacket.

Clarence still can't do much. The kick to his balls still has him down.

Drexl finds it and pulls it out. He flips it open to the driver's license.

Well, well, well, looky what we got here. Clarence Worley. Sounds almost like a nigger name.
                  (*to Clarence*)
Hey, dummy.

He puts his foot on Clarence's chest. Clarence's POV, as he looks up.

Before you brought your dumb ass through the door, I didn't know shit. I just chalked it up to au revoir Alabama. But, because you think you're some macho motherfucker, I know who she's with. You. I know who you are, Clarence Worley. And, I know where you live, 4900 116th Street, apartment 48. And I'll make a million-dollar bet, Alabama's at the same address. Marty, take the car and go get 'er. Bring her dumb ass back here.

He hands Marty the driver's license. Marty goes to get the car keys and a jacket.

> (*to Marty*)
> I'll keep lover boy here entertained.
> (*to Clarence*)
> You know the first thing I think I'll do when she gets here. I think I'll make her suck my dick, and I'll come all in her face. I mean it ain't nuttin' new. She's done it before. But I want you as a audience.
> (*hollering to Marty*)
> Marty, what the fuck are you doin'?

MARTY
(*off*)

I'm tryin' to find my jacket.

DREXL

Look in the hamper. Linda's been dumpin' everybody's stray clothes there lately.

While Drexl has his attention turned to Marty, Clarence reaches into his sock and pulls out the .38. He stick the barrel between Drexl's legs. Drexl, who's standing over Clarence, looks down just in time to see Clarence pull the trigger and blow his balls to bits. Tiny spots of blood speckle Clarence's face.

Drexl shrieks in horror and pain, and falls to the ground.

MARTY
(*off*)

What's happening?

Marty steps into the room.

Clarence doesn't hesitate, he shoots Marty four times in the chest.

Two of the three Hookers have run out of the front door, screaming. The other Hooker is curled up in the corner. She's too stoned to run, but stoned enough to be terrified.

Drexl, still alive, is laying on the ground howling, holding what's left of his balls and dick.

Clarence points the gun at the remaining Hooker.

CLARENCE
Get a bag and put Alabama's things in it!

She doesn't move.

You wanna get shot? I ain't got all fuckin' day, so move it!

The Hooker, tears of fear ruining her mascara, grabs a suitcase from under the bed, and, on her hands and knees, pushes it along the floor to Clarence.

Clarence takes it by the handle and wobbles over to Drexl, who's curled up like a pillbug.

CU – *Clarence's forgotten driver's license in Marty's bloody hand.*

Clarence puts his foot on Drexl's chest.

(*to Drexl*)
Open your eyes, laughing boy.

He doesn't. Clarence gives him a kick.

Open your eyes!

He does. It's now Drexl's POV from on the floor.

You thought it was pretty funny, didn't you?

He fires.

CU – *the bullet comes out of the gun and heads right toward us. When it reaches us, the screen goes awash in red.*

INT. CLARENCE'S APARTMENT – NIGHT

The front door swings open and Clarence walks in. Alabama jumps off the couch and runs toward Clarence, before she reaches him he blurts out:

CLARENCE
I killed him.

She stops short.

I've got some food in the car, I'll be right back.

67

Clarence leaves. Except for the TV playing, the room is quiet. Alabama sits on the couch.

Clarence walks back into the room with a whole bounty of take-out food. He heaps it on to the coffee table and starts to chow down.

Help yourself. I got enough. I am fuckin' starvin'. I think I ordered one of everythin'.

He stops and looks at her.

I am so hungry.

He starts eating french fries and hamburgers.

ALABAMA
(*in a daze*)

Was it him or you?

CLARENCE

Yeah. But to be honest, I put myself in that position. When I drove up there I said to myself, 'If I can kill 'em and get away with it, I'll do it.' I could. So I did.

ALABAMA

Is this a joke?

CLARENCE

No joke. This is probably the best hamburger I've ever had. I'm serious, I've never had a hamburger taste this good.

Alabama starts to cry. Clarence continues eating, ignoring her.

Come on, Bama, eat something. You'll feel better.

She continues crying. He continues eating and ignoring her. Finally he spins on her, yelling:

Why are you crying? He's not worth one of your tears. Would you rather it had been me? Do you love him?
(*no answer*)
Do you love him?
(*no answer*)
Do you love him?

She looks at Clarence, having a hard time getting a word out.

68

ALABAMA

I think what you did was . . .

CLARENCE

What?

ALABAMA

I think what you did . . .

CLARENCE

What?

ALABAMA

I think what you did . . .

CLARENCE

What?

ALABAMA

. . . was so romantic.

Clarence is completely taken aback. They meet in a long, passionate lovers' kiss. Their kiss breaks and slowly the world comes back to normal.

I gotta get outta these clothes.

CLARENCE

I have your things right here.

He picks up the suitcase and drops it on the table in front of them.

ALABAMA
(*comically*)

Clean clothes. There is a God.

Clarence flips open the suitcase. Alabama's and her husband's jaws drop.

Clarence. Those aren't my clothes.

CUT TO:

EXT. HOLLYWOOD HOLIDAY INN – DAY

We see the Hollywood Holiday Inn sign. Pan to the parking lot where Clarence's empty red Mustang is parked.

INT. HOLLYWOOD HOLIDAY INN — CLARENCE'S ROOM — DAY

CU — Dick's jaw drops. His hand reaches out of shot.

CU — The reason for all the jaw dropping . . . the suitcase is full of cocaine! Dick's hand enters frame and fondles a bag.

Clarence smiles, holding a bottle of wine.

Alabama's watching the cable TV.

                         DICK
Holy Mary, Mother of God.

                       ALABAMA
This is great, we got cable.

                      CLARENCE
                    (*to Alabama*)
Bama, you got your blade?

Keeping her eyes on the TV, she pulls out from her purse a Swiss army knife with a tiny dinosaur on it and tosses it to Clarence. Clarence takes off the corkscrew and opens the wine.

He pours some wine into a couple of hotel plastic cups, a big glass for Dick, a little one for himself. He hands it to Dick. Dick takes it and drinks.

                         DICK
This shit can't be real.

                      CLARENCE
It'll get ya high.

He tosses Dick the knife.

Do you want some wine, sweetheart?

                       ALABAMA
Nope. I'm not really a wine gal.

Using the knife, Dick snorts some of the cocaine. He jumps back.

                         DICK
It's fuckin' real!
                     (*to Clarence*)
It's fuckin' real!

70

                    CLARENCE
I certainly hope so.

                      DICK
You've got a helluva lotta coke there, man!

                    CLARENCE
I know.

                      DICK
Do you have any idea how much fuckin' coke you got?

                    CLARENCE
Tell me.

                      DICK
I don't know! A fuckin' lot!

He downs his wine. Clarence fills his glass.

This is Drexl's coke!?

                    CLARENCE
Drexl's dead. This is Clarence's coke and Clarence can do
whatever he wants with it. And what Clarence wants to do is sell
it. Then me and Bama are gonna leave on a jet plane and spend the
rest of our lives spendin'. So, you got my letter, have you lined up
any buyers?

                      DICK
Look, Clarence, I'm not Joe Cocaine.

Dick gulps half of his wine. Clarence fills it up.

                    CLARENCE
But you're an actor. I hear these Hollywood guys have it delivered
to the set.

                      DICK
Yeah, they do. And maybe when I start being a successful actor
I'll know those guys. But most of the people I know are like me.
They ain't got a pot to piss in or a window to throw it out of. Now,
if you want to sell a little bit at a time –

71

CLARENCE

No way! The whole enchilada in one shot.

DICK

Do you have any idea how difficult that's gonna be?

CLARENCE

I'm offering a half a million dollars' worth of white for two hundred thousand. How difficult can that be?

DICK

It's difficult because you're sellin' it to a particular group. Big shots. Fat cats. Guys who can use that kind of quantity. Guys who can afford two hundred thousand. Basically, guys I don't know. You don't know. And, more important, they don't know you. I did talk with one guy who could possibly help you.

CLARENCE

Is he big league?

DICK

He's nothing. He's in my acting class. But he works as an assistant to a very powerful movie producer named Lee Donowitz. I thought Donowitz could be interested in a deal like this. He could use it. He could afford it.

CLARENCE

What'd'ya tell 'em?

DICK

Hardly anything. I wasn't sure from your letter what was bullshit, and what wasn't.

CLARENCE

What's this acting class guy's name?

DICK

Elliot.

CLARENCE

Elliot what?

DICK

Elliot Blitzer.

CLARENCE

OK, call 'im up and arrange a meeting, so we can get through all the getting to know you stuff.

DICK

Where?

CLARENCE
(*to Alabama*)

Where?

ALABAMA

The zoo.

CLARENCE
(*to Dick*)

The zoo.
(*pause*)
What are you waiting for?

DICK

Would you just shut up a minute and let me think?

CLARENCE

What's to think about?

DICK

Shut up! First you come waltzing into my life after two years. You're married. You killed a guy.

CLARENCE

Two guys.

DICK

Two guys. Now you want me to help you with some big drug deal. Fuck, Clarence, you killed somebody and you're blowin' it off like it don't mean shit.

CLARENCE

Don't expect me to be all broken up over poor Drexl. I think he was a fuckin', freeloadin', parasitic scumbag, and he got exactly what he deserved. I got no pity for a mad dog like that. I think I should get a merit badge or somethin'.

73

Dick rests his head in his hands.

Look, buddy, I realize I'm layin' some pretty heavy shit on ya, but I need you to rise to the occasion. So, drink some more wine. Get used to the idea, and get your friend on the phone.

EXT. LOS ANGELES ZOO – DAY

CU – A black panther, the four-legged kind, paces back and forth.

Clarence, Alabama, Dick, and Elliot Blitzer are walking through the zoo. One look at Elliot and you can see what type of actor he is, a real GQ, blow-dry boy. As they walk and talk, Clarence is eating a box of animal crackers and Alabama is blowing soap bubbles.

> ELLIOT
> So you guys got five hundred thousand dollars' worth of cola that you're unloading –

> CLARENCE
> Want an animal cracker?

> ELLIOT
> Yeah, OK.

He takes one.

> CLARENCE
> Leave the gorillas.

> ELLIOT
> – that you're unloading for two hundred thousand dollars –

> CLARENCE
> Unloading? That's a helluva way to describe the bargain of a lifetime.

> DICK
> (*trying to chill him out*)
> Clarence . . .

> ELLIOT
> Where did you get it?

CLARENCE

I grow it on my window-sill. The light's really great there and I'm up high enough so you can't see it from the street.

ELLIOT
(*forcing a laugh*)
Ha ha ha. No really, where does it come from?

CLARENCE

Coco leaves. You see, they take the leaves and mash it down until it's kind of a paste –

ELLIOT
(*turning to Dick*)
Look, Dick, I don't –

CLARENCE
(*laughing*)
No problem, Elliot. I'm just fuckin' wit ya, that's all. Actually, I'll tell you but you gotta keep it quiet. Understand, if Dick didn't assure me you're good people I'd just tell ya, none of your fuckin' business. But, as a sign of good faith, here it goes: I gotta friend in the department.

ELLIOT

What department?

CLARENCE

What do you think, eightball?

ELLIOT

The police department?

CLARENCE

Duh. What else would I be talking about? Now stop askin' stupid doorknob questions. Well, a year and a half ago, this friend of mine got access to the evidence room for an hour. He snagged this coke. But, he's a good cop with a wife and a kid, so he sat on it for a year and a half until he found a guy he could trust.

ELLIOT

He trusts you?

CLARENCE

We were in Four H together. We've known each other since childhood. So, I'm handling the sales part. He's my silent partner, and he knows if I get fucked up, I won't drop dime on him. He's kinda paranoid. Now, no farther, you understand. I didn't tell you nothin' and you didn't hear nothin'.

ELLIOT

Sure. I didn't hear anything.

Elliot is more than satisfied. Clarence makes a comical face at Dick when Elliot's not looking. Dick is wearing an I-don't-believe-this-guy expression. Alabama is forever blowing bubbles.

CUT TO:

EXT. LOS ANGELES ZOO – SNACK BAR – DAY

We're in the snack bar area of the zoo. Alabama, Dick, and Elliot are sitting around a plastic outdoor table. Clarence is pacing around the table as he talks. Alabama is still blowing bubbles.

CLARENCE
(*to Elliot*)

Do I look like a beautiful blond with big tits and an ass that tastes like French vanilla ice-cream?

Elliot hasn't the slightest idea what that is supposed to mean.

ELLIOT

What?

CLARENCE

Do I look like a beautiful blond with big tits and an ass that tastes like French vanilla ice-cream?

ELLIOT
(*with conviction*)

No. No, you don't.

CLARENCE

Then why are you telling me all this bullshit just so you can fuck me?

76

                              DICK
                      (*trying to chill him out*)
Clarence . . .

                            CLARENCE
                           (*to Dick*)
Let me handle this.

                             ELLIOT
Get it straight, Lee isn't into taking risks. He deals with a couple of
guys, and he's been dealing with them for years. They're reliable.
They're dependable. And, they're safe.

                            CLARENCE
Riddle me this, Batman. If you're all so much in love with each
other, what the fuck are you doing here? I'm sure you got better
things to do with your time than walk around in circles starin' up a
panther's ass. Your guy's interested because with that much shit at
his fingertips he can play Joe fuckin' Hollywood till the wheels
come off. He can sell it, he can snort it, he can play Santa Claus with
it. At the price he's payin', he'll have the freedom to be able to just
throw it around. He'll be everybody's best friend. And, you know,
that's what we're talkin' about here. I'm not puttin' him down.
Hey, let him run wild. Have a ball, it's his money. But, don't expect
me to hang around forever waitin' for you guys to grow some guts.

Elliot has been silenced. He nods his head in agreement.

INT. PORSCHE – MOVING – MULHOLLAND DRIVE – DAY

*Movie producer, Lee Donowitz, is driving his Porsche through the winding
Hollywood hills, just enjoying being rich and powerful. His cellular car
phone rings, he answers.*

                              LEE
Hello.
                             (*pause*)
Elliot, it's Sunday. Why am I talkin' to you on Sunday? I don't see
enough of you during the week I gotta talk to you on Sunday? Why
is it you always call me when I'm on the windiest street in LA?

BACK TO: ELLIOT

Elliot is on the zoo payphone. Clarence is next to him. Dick is next to Clarence. Alabama is next to Dick, blowing bubbles.

> ELLIOT
> (*on phone*)
> I'm with that party you wanted me to get together with. Do you know what I'm talking about, Lee?

BACK TO: LEE

Store-fronts whiz by in the background.

> LEE
> Why the hell are you calling my phone to talk about that?

BACK TO: ELLIOT

> ELLIOT
> Well, he's here right now, and he insists on talking to you.

BACK TO: LEE

In the 7th Street tunnel. Lee's voice echoes.

> LEE
> Are you outta your fuckin' mind?

BACK TO: ELLIOT

> ELLIOT
> You said if I didn't get you on the –

Clarence takes the receiver out of Elliot's hand.

> CLARENCE
> (*into phone*)
> Hello, Lee, it's Clarence. At last we meet.

EXT. DICK'S APARTMENT – DAY

Virgil's knocking on Dick's door. Floyd (Dick's room-mate) answers.

> VIRGIL
> Hello, is Dick Ritchie here?

FLOYD

Naw, he ain't home right now.

VIRGIL

Do you live here?

FLOYD

Yeah, I live here.

VIRGIL

Sorta room-mates?

FLOYD

Exactly room-mates.

VIRGIL

Maybe you can help me. Actually, who I'm looking for is a friend
of ours from Detroit. Clarence Worley? I heard he was in town.
Might be traveling with a pretty girl named Alabama. Have you
seen him? Are they stayin' here?

FLOYD

Naw, they ain't stayin' here. But, I know who you're talkin'
about. They're stayin' at the Hollywood Holiday Inn.

VIRGIL

How do you know? You been there?

FLOYD

No, I ain't been there. But I heard him say it. Hollywood Holiday
Inn. Kinda easy to remember.

VIRGIL

You're right. It is.

EXT. LOS ANGELES ZOO – PAYPHONE – DAY

Clarence is still on the phone with Lee.

CLARENCE

Lee, the reason I'm talkin' with you is I want to open *Doctor
Zhivago* in LA. And I want you to distribute it.

BACK TO: LEE

Stopped in traffic on Sunset Boulevard.

LEE

I don't know, Clarence, *Doctor Zhivago*'s a pretty big movie.

BACK TO: CLARENCE

CLARENCE

The biggest. The biggest movie you've ever dealt with, Lee. We're talkin' a lot of film. A man'd have ta be an idiot not to be a little cautious about a movie like that. And Lee, you're no idiot.

BACK TO: LEE

He's still stuck on Sunset Boulevard, the traffic's moving better now.

LEE

I'm not sayin' I'm not interested. But being a distributor's not what I'm all about. I'm a film producer, I'm on this world to make good movies. Nothing more. Now, having my big toe dipped into the distribution end helps me on many levels.

Traffic breaks and Lee speeds along. The background whizzes past him.

But the bottom line is: I'm not Paramount. I have a select group of distributors I deal with. I buy their little movies. Accomplish what I wanna accomplish, end of story. Easy, business-like, very little risk.

BACK TO: CLARENCE

CLARENCE

Now that's bullshit, Lee. Every time you buy one of those little movies it's a risk. I'm not sellin' you something that's gonna play two weeks, six weeks, then go straight to cable. This is *Doctor Zhivago*. This'll be packin' 'em in for a year and a half. Two years! That's two years you don't have to work with anybody's movie but mine.

BACK TO: LEE

Speeding down a beachside road.

LEE

Well then, what's the hurry? Is it true the rights to *Doctor Zhivago* are in arbitration?

80

BACK TO: CLARENCE

CLARENCE

I wanna be able to announce this deal at Cannes. If I had time for a courtship, Lee, I would. I'd take ya out, I'd hold your hand, I'd kiss you on the cheek at the door. But, I'm not in that position. I need to know if we're in bed together, or not. If you want my movie, Lee, you're just gonna have to come to terms with your Fear and Desire.

Pause. Clarence hands the phone to Elliot.

(*to Elliot*)

He wants ta talk to ya.

ELLIOT
(*into phone*)

Mr Donowitz?

(*pause*)

I told you, through Dick.

(*pause*)

He's in my acting class.

(*pause*)

About a year.

(*pause*)

Yeah, he's good.

(*pause*)

They grew up together.

(*pause*)

Sure thing.

Elliot hangs up the phone.

He says Wednesday at three o'clock at the Beverly Wilshire. He wants everybody there.
(*pointing at Clarence*)
He'll talk to you. If after talkin' to you he's convinced you're OK, he'll do business. If not, he'll say fuck it and walk out the door. He also wants a sample bag.

CLARENCE

No problem on both counts.

He offers Elliot the animal crackers.

Have a cookie.

Elliot takes one.

                        ELLIOT
Thanks.

He puts in in his mouth.

                        CLARENCE
That wasn't a gorilla, was it?

EXT. HOLIDAY INN – DAY

*The red Mustang with Clarence and Alabama pulls up to the hotel.
Alabama hops out. Clarence stays in.*

                        ALABAMA
You did it, Quickdraw, I'm so proud of you. You were like a
ninja. Did I do my part OK?

                        CLARENCE
Babalouey, you were perfect, I could hardly keep from busting
up.

                        ALABAMA
I felt so stupid just blowing those bubbles.

                        CLARENCE
You were chillin', kind of creepy even. You totally fucked with his
head. I'm gonna go grab dinner.

                        ALABAMA
I'm gonna hop in the tub and get all wet, and slippery, and soapy.
Then I'm gonna lie in the waterbed, not even both to dry off, and
watch X-rated movies till you get your ass back to my lovin' arms.

They kiss.

                        CLARENCE
We now return you to *Bullit* already in progress.

He slams the Mustang in reverse and peels out of the hotel. Alabama walks her little walk from the parking lot to the pool area. Somebody whistles at her, she turns to them.

ALABAMA

Thank you.

She gets to her door, takes out the key, and opens her door.

INT. HOLLYWOOD HOLIDAY INN – CLARENCE'S ROOM – DAY

She steps in only to find Virgil sitting in a chair placed in front of the door with a sawed-off shutgun aimed right at her.

VIRGIL
(*calmly*)

Step inside and shut the door.

She doesn't move, she's frozen. Virgil leans forward.

(*calmly*)

Lady. I'm gonna shoot you in the face.

She does exactly as he says. Virgil rises, still aiming the sawed-off.

Step away from the door, move into the room.

She does. He puts the shotgun down on the chair, then steps closer to her.

OK, Alabama, where's our coke, where's Clarence, and when's he coming back.

ALABAMA

I think you got the wrong room, my name is Sadie. I don't have any Coke, but there's a Pepsi machine downstairs. I don't know any Clarence, but maybe my husband does. You might have heard of him, he plays football, Al Lylezado. He'll be home any minute, you can ask him.

Virgil can't help but smile.

VIRGIL

You're cute.

Virgil jumps up and does a mid-air kung fu kick which catches Alabama square in the face, lifting her off the ground and dropping her flat on her back.

INT. MOVING RED MUSTANG – DAY

Clarence, in his car, driving to get something to eat, singing to himself.

> CLARENCE
> (*singing*)
> 'Land of stardust, land of glamour,
> Vistavision and Cinerama,
> Everything about it is a must,
> To get to Hollywood, or bust . . .'

INT. HOLLYWOOD HOLIDAY INN – CLARENCE'S ROOM – DAY

Alabama's laying flat. She actually blacks out for a moment, but the salty taste of the blood in her mouth wakes her up. She opens her eyes and sees Virgil standing there, smiling. She closes them, hoping it's a dream. They open again to the same sight. She has never felt more helpless in her life.

> VIRGIL
> Hurts, don't it? It better. Took me a long time to kick like that. I'm a third-degree blackbelt, you know? At home I got trophies. Tournaments I was in. Kicked all kinds of ass. I got great technique. You ain't hurt that bad. Get on your feet, Fruitloop.

Alabama wobbily complies.

> Where's our coke? Where's Clarence? And when's he comin' back?

Alabama looks in Virgil's eyes and realizes that without a doubt she's going to die, because this man is going to kill her.

> ALABAMA
> Go take a flying fuck at a rolling donut.

Virgil doesn't waste a second. He gives her a side kick straight to the stomach. The air is sucked out of her lungs. She falls to her knees. She's on all fours gasping for air that's just not there.

Virgil whips out a pack of Lucky Strikes. He lights one up with a Zippo lighter. He takes a long, deep drag.

Whatsamatta? Can't breathe? Get used to it.

INT. HAMBURGER STAND – DAY

Clarence walks through the door of some mom and pop fast-food restaurant.

CLARENCE
Woah! Smells like hamburgers in here! What's the biggest, fattest hamburger you guys got?

The Iranian Guy at the counter says:

IRANIAN GUY
That would be Steve's double chili cheeseburger.

CLARENCE
Well, I want two of them bad boys. Two large orders of chili fries. Two large Diet Cokes.
(*looking at menu on wall*)
And I'll tell you what, why don't you give me a combination burrito as well.

INT. HOLLYWOOD HOLIDAY INN – CLARENCE'S ROOM – DAY

Alabama is violently thrown into a corner of the room. She braces herself against the walls. She is very punchy. Virgil steps in front of her.

VIRGIL
You think your boyfriend would go through this kind of shit for you? Dream on, cunt. You're nothin' but a fuckin' fool. And your pretty face is gonna turn awful goddamn ugly in about two seconds. Now where's my fuckin' coke?

She doesn't answer. He delivers a spinning roundhouse kick to the head. Her head slams into the left side of the wall.

Where's Clarence?!

Nothing. He gives her another kick to the head, this time from the other side. Her legs start to give way. He catches her and throws her back. He slaps her lightly in the face to revive her, she looks at him.

85

When's Clarence getting back?

She can barely raise her arm, but she somehow manages, and she gives him the middle finger. Virgil can't help but smile.

You gotta lot of heart, kid.

He gives her a spinning roundhouse kick to the head that sends her to the floor.

INT. HAMBURGER STAND – DAY

CU – Burgers sizzling on a griddle. Chili and cheese is put on them.

Clarence is waiting for his order. He notices a Customer reading a copy of Newsweek *with Elvis on the cover.*

                    CLARENCE
That's a great issue.

The Customer lowers his magazine a little bit.

                    CUSTOMER
Yeah, I subscribe. It's a pretty decent one.

                    CLARENCE
Have you read the story on Elvis.

                    CUSTOMER
No. Not yet.

                    CLARENCE
You know, I saw it on the stands, my first inclination was to buy it. But, I look at the price and say forget it, it's just gonna be the same old shit. I ended up breaking down and buying it a few days later. Man, was I ever wrong.

                    CUSTOMER
Liked it, huh?

                    CLARENCE
It's probably the single best piece I've ever read about Elvis in my life.

86

CUSTOMER

That good, huh?

He takes the magazine from the Customer's hands and starts flipping to the Elvis article.

CLARENCE

It tried to pin down what the attraction is after all these years. It covers the whole spectrum of fans, the people who love his music, the people who grew up with him, the artists he inspired – Bob Dylan, Bruce Springsteen, and the fanatics, like these guys. I don't know about you, but they give me the creeps.

CUSTOMER

I can see what you mean.

CLARENCE

Like, look at her. She looks like she fell off of an ugly tree and hit every branch on the way down. Elvis wouldn't fuck her with Pat Boone's dick.

Clarence and the Customer laugh.

INT. HOLLYWOOD HOLIDAY INN – CLARENCE'S ROOM – DAY

Alabama's pretty beat up. She has a fat lip and her face is black and blue. She's crawling around on the floor. Virgil is tearing the place apart looking for the cocaine. He's also carrying on a running commentary.

VIRGIL

Now the first guy you kill is always the hardest. I don't care if you're the Boston Strangler or Wyatt Earp. You can bet that Texas boy, Charles Whitman, the fella who shot all them guys from that tower, I'll bet you green money that that first little black dot that he took a bead on, was the bitch of the bunch. No foolin', the first one's a tough row to hoe. Now, the second one, while it ain't no Mardi Gras, it ain't half as tough as the first. You still feel somethin' but it's just so diluted this time around. Then you completely level off on the third one. The third one's easy. It's gotten to the point now I'll do it just to watch their expression change.

87

He's tearing the motel room up in general. Then he flips the mattress up off the bed, and the black suitcase is right there.

Alabama is crawling, unnoticed, to where her purse is lying.

Virgil flips open the black case and almost goes snowblind.

> Well, well, well, looky here. I guess I just reached journey's end. Great. One less thing I gotta worry about.

Virgil closes the case. Alabama sifts through her purse.

She pulls out her Swiss army knife, opens it up. Virgil turns toward her.

VIRGIL
> OK, Sugarpop, we've come to what I like to call the moment of truth –

Alabama slowly rises clutching the thrust-out knife in both hands. Mr Karate-man smiles.

> Kid, you gotta lot a heart.

He moves toward her.

Alabama's hands are shaking.

> Tell you what I'm gonna do. I'm gonna give you a free swing. Now, I only do that for people I like.

He moves close.

Alabama's eyes study him. He grabs the front of his shirt and rips it open. Buttons fly everywhere.

> Go ahead, girl, take a stab at it.
>> (*giggling*)
> You don't have anything to lose.

CU – Alabama's face. Virgil's right, she doesn't have anything to lose. Virgil's also right about this being the moment of truth. The ferocity in women that comes out at certain times, and is just there under the surface in many women all of the time, is unleashed. The absolute feeling of helplessness she felt only a moment ago has taken a one hundred and eighty degree turn into 'I'll take this motherfucker with me if it's the last thing I do' seething hatred.

88

Letting out a bloodcurdling yell, she raises the knife high above her head, then drops to her knees and plunges it deep into Virgil's right foot.

CU – Virgil's face. Talk about bloodcurdling yells.

Alabama is kicked in the teeth with Virgil's left foot.

Virgil bends down and carefully pulls the knife from his foot, tears running down his face.

While Virgil's bent down, Alabama smashes an Elvis Presley whiskey decanter that Clarence bought her in Oklahoma over his head. It's only made of plaster, so it doesn't kill him.

Virgil's moving toward Alabama, limping on his bad foot.

> VIRGIL

OK, no more Mr Nice-guy.

Alabama picks up the hotel TV and tosses it to him. He instinctively catches it and, with his arms full of television, Alabama cold-cocks him with her fist in his nose, breaking it.

Her eyes go straight to the door, then to the sawed-off shotgun by it. She runs to it, bends over the chair for the gun. Virgil's left foot kicks her in the back, sending her flying over the chair and smashing into the door.

Virgil furiously throws the chair out of the way and stands over Alabama. Alabama's lying on the ground laughing. Virgil has killed a lot of people, but not one of them has ever laughed before he did it.

> VIRGIL

What's so funny?!!

> ALABAMA
> (*laughing*)

You look so ridiculous.

She laughs louder. Virgil's insane. He picks her off the floor, then lifts her off the ground and throws her through the glass shower door in the bathroom.

> VIRGIL

Laugh it up, cunt. You were in hysterics a minute ago. Why ain't you laughing now?

Alabama, lying in the bathtub, grabs a small bottle of hotel shampoo and squeezes it out in her hand.

Virgil reaches in the shower and grabs hold of her hair.

Alabama rubs the shampoo in his face. He lets go of her and his hands go to his eyes.

Oh Jesus!

She grabs hold of a hefty piece of broken glass and plunges it into his face.

Oh Mary, help me!

The battered and bruised and bloody Alabama emerges from the shower. She's clutching a big, bloody piece of broken glass. She's vaguely reminiscent of a Tasmanian devil. Poor Virgil can't see very well, but he sees her figure coming toward him. He lets out a wild haymaker that catches her in the jaw and knocks her into the toilet.

She recovers almost immediately and takes the porcelain lid off the back of the toilet tank.

Virgil whips out a .45 automatic from his shoulder holster, just as Alabama brings the lid down on his head. He's pressed up against the wall with this toilet lid hitting him. He can't get a good shot in this tight environment, but he fires anyway, hitting the floor, the wall, the toilet, and the sink.

The toilet lid finally shatters against Virgil's head. He falls to the ground.

Alabama goes to the medicine cabinet and whips out a big can of Final Net hairspray. She pulls a Bic lighter out of her pocket, and, just as Virgil raises his gun at her, she flicks the Bic and sends a stream of hairspray through the flame, which results in a big ball of fire that hits Virgil right in the face.

He fires off two shots. One hits the wall, another hits the sink pipe, sending water spraying.

Upon getting his face fried Virgil screams and jumps up, knocking Alabama down, and runs out of the bathroom.

Virgil collapses on to the floor of the living room. Then, he sees the sawed-off laying on the ground. He crawls toward it.

Alabama, in the bathroom, sees where he's heading. She picks up the .45 automatic and fires at him. It's empty. She's on her feet and into the room.

He reaches the shotgun, his hands grasp it.

Alabama spots and picks up the bloody Swiss army knife. She takes a knife-first running-dive at Virgil's back. She hits him.

He arches up, firing the sawed-off into the ceiling, dropping the gun, and sending a cloud of plaster and stucco all over the room.

Alabama snatches the shotgun.

Arched over on his back Virgil and Alabama make eye contact.

The first blast hits him in the shoulder, almost tearing his arm off. The second hits him in the knee. The third plays hell with his chest.

Alabama then runs at him, hitting him in the head with the butt of the shotgun.

Ever since she's been firing it's as if some other part of her brain has been functioning independently. She's been absent-mindedly saying the prayer of Saint Francis of Assisi.

ALABAMA
Lord, make me an instrument of Thy peace;
where there is hatred, let me sow love;
where there is injury, pardon;
where there is doubt, faith;
where there is despair, hope;
where there is darkness, light;
and where there is sadness, joy.
  O Divine Master, grant that I may not
so much seek to be consoled as to console;
to be understod as to understand;
to be loved, as to love;
for it is in giving that we receive,
it is in pardoning that we are pardoned,
and it is in dying that we are born
to eternal life.

Clarence, who's been hearing gunshots, bursts through the door, gun drawn, only to see Alabama, hitting a dead guy on the head, with a shotgun.

CLARENCE

Honey?

She continues. He puts his gun away.

Sweetheart? Cops are gonna be here any minute.

She continues. He takes the gun away from her, and she falls to the ground. She lies on the floor trembling, continuing with the downward swings of her arms.

Clarence grabs the shotgun and the cocaine, and tosses Alabama over his shoulder.

CUT TO:

EXT. HOLLYWOOD HOLIDAY INN – DAY

Everybody is outside their rooms watching as Clarence walks through the pool area with his bundle. Sirens can be heard.

EXT. MOVING RED MUSTANG – DAY

Clarence is driving like mad. Alabama's passed out in the passenger seat. She's muttering to herself. Clarence has one hand on the steering wheel and the other strokes Alabama's hair.

CLARENCE

Sleep baby. Don't dream. Don't worry. Just sleep. You deserve better than this. I'm so sorry. Sleep my angel. Sleep peacefully.

EXT. MOTEL 6 – NIGHT

A new motel. Clarence's red Mustang is parked outside.

INT. MOTEL 6 – CLARENCE'S ROOM– NIGHT

Alabama, with a fat lip and a black and blue face, is asleep in bed.

INT. NOWHERE

Clarence is in a nondescript room speaking directly to camera. He's in a headshot.

CLARENCE

I feel so horrible about what she went through. That fucker really beat the shit out of her. She never told him where I was. It's like I always felt that the way she felt about me was a mistake. She couldn't really care that much. I always felt in the back of my mind, I don't know, she was jokin'. But, to go through that and remain loyal, it's very easy to be enraptured with words, but to remain loyal when it's easier, even excusable, not to – that's a test of oneself. That's true romance. I swear to God, I'll cut off my hands and gouge out my eyes before I'll ever let anything happen to that lady again.

CUT TO:

EXT. HOLLYWOOD HILLS – NIGHT

A wonderful, gracefully flowing shot of the Hollywood hills. Off in the distance we hear the roar of a car engine.

EXT. MULHOLLAND DRIVE – NIGHT

Vaaaarrrooooooommmm!!! A silver Porsche is driving hells bells, taking quick corners, pushing it to the edge.

INT. MOVING SILVER PORSCHE – NIGHT

Elliot Blitzer is the driver, standing on it. A blond, glitzy Coke Whore is sitting next to him. They're having a ball. Then they see a red and blue light flashing in the rear-view mirror. It's the cops.

ELLIOT

Fuck! I knew it! I knew it! I fucking knew it! I should have my head examined, driving like this!
                    (*he pulls over*)
Kandi, you gotta help me.

KANDI

What can I do?

He pulls out the sample bag of cocaine that Clarence gave him earlier.

ELLIOT

You gotta hold this for me.

KANDI

You must be high. Uh-uh. No way.

ELLIOT
(*frantically*)

Just put it in your purse!

KANDI

I'm not gonna put that shit in my purse.

ELLIOT

They won't search you, I promise. You haven't done anything.

KANDI

No way, José.

ELLIOT

Please, they'll be here any minute. Just put it in your bra.

KANDI

I'm not wearing a bra.

ELLIOT
(*pleading*)

Put it in your pants.

KANDI

No.

ELLIOT

You're the one who wanted to drive fast.

KANDI

Read my lips.

She mouths the word 'no'.

ELLIOT

After all I've done for you, you fucking whore!!

She goes to slap him, she hits the bag of cocaine instead. It rips open. Cocaine completely covers his blue suit. At that moment Elliot turns to face a flashlight beam. Tears fill his eyes.

94

INT. POLICE STATION – INTERROGATION ROOM – DAY

Elliot is sitting in a chair at a table. Two young, good-looking, casually dressed, Starsky and Hutch-*type Police Detectives are questioning him. They're known in the department as Nicholson and Dimes. The dark-haired one is Cody Nicholson, and the blond is Nicky Dimes.*

NICHOLSON

Look, sunshine, we found a sandwich bag of uncut cocaine –

DIMES

Not a tiny little vial –

NICHOLSON

But a fuckin' baggie.

DIMES

Now don't sit there and feed us some shit.

NICHOLSON

You got caught. It's all fun and fuckin' games till you get caught. But now we gottcha. OK, Mr Elliot actor, you've just made the big time –

DIMES

You're no longer an extra –

NICHOLSON

Or a bit player –

DIMES

Or a supporting actor –

NICHOLSON

You're a fuckin' star! And you're gonna be playin' your little one-man show nightly for the next two fuckin' years for a captive audience –

DIMES

But there is a bright side though. If you ever have to play a part of a guy who gets fucked in his ass on a daily basis by throat-slitting niggers, you'll have so much experience to draw on –

NICHOLSON

And just think, when you get out in a few years, you'll meet some

95

girl, get married, and you'll be so understanding to your wife's needs, because you'll know what it's like to be a woman –

NICHOLSON

DIMES

'Course you'll wanna fuck her in the ass. Pussy just won't feel right anymore –

NICHOLSON

That is, of course, if you don't catch Aids from all your anal intrusions.

Elliot starts crying. Nicholson and Dimes exchange looks and smiles. Mission accomplished.

INT. POLICE STATION – CAPTAIN KRINKLE'S OFFICE – DAY

Captain Bufford Krinkle is sitting behind his desk, where he spends about seventy-five percent of his days. He's your standard rough, gruff, no-nonsense, by-the-book-type police captain.

KRINKLE

Nicholson! Dimes! Get in here!

The two casually dressed, sneaker-wearing cops rush in, both shouting at once.

NICHOLSON

Krinkle, this is it. We got it, man. And it's all ours. I mean talk about fallin' into somethin'. You shoulda seen it, it was beautiful. Dimes is hittin' him from the left about being fucked in the ass by niggers, I'm hittin' him from the right about not likin' pussy anymore, finally he just starts cryin', and then it was all over –

DIMES

Krinkle, you're lookin' at the two future cops of the month. We have it, and when I say we, I don't mean me and him, I'm referring to the whole department. Haven't had a decent bust this whole month. Well, we mighta come in like a lamb, but we're goin' out like a lion –

KRINKLE

Both you idiots, shut up, I can't understand shit! Now, what's happened, what's going on, and what are you talking about?

Okee-dokee. It's like this, Krinkle; a patrol car stops this dork for
speeding, they walk up to the window and the guy's covered in
coke. So they bring his ass in and me an' Nicholson go to work on
him –

NICHOLSON

Nicholson and I.

DIMES

Nicholson and I go to work on him. Now we know something's
rotten in Denmark, 'cause this dickhead had a big bag, and it's
uncut too, so we're sweatin' him, tryin' to find out where he got it.
Scarin' the shit outta him –

NICHOLSON

Which wasn't too hard, the guy was a real squid.

DIMES

So we got this guy scared shitless and he starts talkin'. And,
Krinkle, you ain't gonna fuckin' believe it.

CUT TO:

INT. RESTAURANT – DAY

*Detroit. Very fancy restaurant. Four wise-guy Hoods, one older, the other
three, youngsters, are seated at a table with Mr Coccotti.*

COCCOTTI

– And so, tomorrow morning comes, and no Virgil. I check with
Nick Cardella, who Virgil was supposed to leave my narcotics
with, he never shows. Now, children, somebody is stickin' a
red-hot poker up my asshole and what I don't know is whose
hand's on the handle.

YOUNG WISE-GUY #1 (FRANKIE)

You think Virgil started gettin' big ideas?

COCCOTTI

It's possible. Anybody can be carried away with delusions of
grandeur. But after that incident in Ann Arbor, I trust Virgil.

YOUNG WISE-GUY #2 (DARIO)

What happened?

OLD WISE-GUY (LENNY)

Virgil got picked up in a warehouse shakedown. He got five years, he served three.

COCCOTTI

Anybody who clams up and does his time, I don't care how I feel about him personally, he's OK.

BACK TO: KRINKLE'S OFFICE

NICHOLSON

It seems a cop from some department, we don't know where, stole a half a million dollars of coke from the property cage and he's been sittin' on it for a year and a half. Now the cops got this weirdo –

DIMES

Suspect's words –

NICHOLSON

To front for him. So Elliot is workin' out a deal between them and his boss, a big movie producer named Lee Donowitz.

DIMES

He produced *Comin' Home in a Body Bag*.

KRINKLE

That Vietnam movie?

NICHOLSON

Uh-huh.

KRINKLE

That was a good fuckin' movie.

DIMES

Sure was.

KRINKLE

Do you believe him?

NICHOLSON

I believe he believes him.

DIMES

He's so spooked he'd turn over his momma, his daddy, his two-panny granny, and Anna and the King of Siam if he had anything on him.

NICHOLSON

This rabbit'll do anything not to do time, including wearing a wire.

KRINKLE

He'll wear a wire?

DIMES

We talked him into it.

KRINKLE

Dirty cops. We'll have to bring in internal affairs on this.

NICHOLSON

Look, we don't care if you bring in the state militia, the volunteer fire department, the LA Thunderbirds, the ghost of Steve McQueen, and twelve Roman gladiators, so long as we get credit for the bust.

DIMES

Cocaine. Dirty cops. Hollywood. This is Crocket and Tubbs all the way. And we found it, so we want the fucking collar.

BACK TO:

INT. RESTAURANT – DAY

YOUNG WISE-GUY #3 (MARVIN)

Maybe Virgil dropped it off at Cardella's. Cardella turns Virgil's switch to off, and Cardella decides to open up his own fruit stand.

LENNY

Excuse me, Mr Coccotti.
(to Marvin)
Do you know Nick Cardella?

MARVIN

No.

LENNY

Then where the hell do you get off talkin' that kind of talk – ?

MARVIN

I didn't mean –

LENNY

Shut your mouth. Nick Cardella was provin' what his word was worth before you were in your daddy's nutsack. What sun do you walk under you can throw a shadow on Nick Cardella? Nick Cardella's a stand-up guy.

COCCOTTI

Children, we're digressing. Another possibility is that rat-fuck whore and her wack-a-doo cowboy boyfriend out-aped Virgil. Knowing Virgil, I find that hard to believe. But they sent Drexl to hell, and Drexl was no faggot. So you see, children, I got a lot of questions and no answers. Find out who this wing-and-a-prayer artist is and take him off at the neck.

TITLE CARD:

'THE BIG DAY'

EXT. IMPERIAL HIGHWAY – SUNRISE

Clarence's red Mustang is parked on top of a hill just off of Imperial Highway. As luck would have it, somebody has abandoned a ratty old sofa on the side of the road. Clarence and Alabama sit on the sofa, sharing a Jumbo Java, and enjoying the sunrise and wonderful view of the LAX Airport runways, where planes are taking off and landing. A plane takes off, and they stop and watch.

CLARENCE

Ya know, I used to fuckin' hate airports.

ALABAMA

Really?

CLARENCE

With a vengeance, I hated them.

ALABAMA

How come?

CLARENCE

I used to live by one back in Dearborn. It's real frustratin' to be surrounded by airplanes when you ain't got shit. I hated where I was, but I couldn't do anythin' about it. I didn't have any money. It was tough enough just tryin' to pay my rent every month, an' here I was livin' next to an airport. Whenever I went outside, I saw fuckin' planes takin' off. I'm tryin' to watch TV, fuckin' planes takin' off drownin' out my show. All day long I'm seein', hearin' people doin' what I wanted to do most, but couldn't.

ALABAMA

What?

CLARENCE

Leavin' Detroit. Goin' off on vacations, startin' new lives, business trips. Fun, fun, fun, fun.

Another plane takes off.

But knowin' me and you gonna be nigger-rich gives me a whole new outlook. I love airports now. Me 'n' you can get on any one of those planes out there, and go anywhere we want.

ALABAMA

You ain't kiddin', we got lives to start over, we should go somewhere where we can really start from scratch.

CLARENCE

I been in America all my life. I'm due for a change. I wanna see what TV in other countries is like. Besides, it's more dramatic. Where should we fly off to, my little turtledove?

ALABAMA

Cancoon.

CLARENCE

Why Cancoon?

ALABAMA

It's got a nice ring to it. It sounds like a movie. *Clarence and Alabama Go to Cancoon.* Don'cha think?

CLARENCE

But in my movie, baby, you get top billing.

They kiss.

Don't you worry 'bout anythin. It's all gonna work out for us. We deserve it.

INT. DICK'S APARTMENT – DAY

Dick, Clarence and Alabama are just getting ready to leave for the drug deal. Floyd lays on the couch watching TV. Alabama's wearing dark glasses because of the black eye she has.

CLARENCE
(*to Floyd*)

You sure that's how you get to the Beverly Wilshire?

FLOYD

I've partied there twice. Yeah, I'm sure.

DICK

Yeah, well if we get lost, it's your ass.
(*to Clarence*)
Come on, Clarence, let's go. Elliot's going to meet us in the lobby.

CLARENCE

I'm just makin' sure we got everything.
(*pointing to Alabama*)
You got yours?

She holds up the suitcase. The phone rings. The three pile out the door. Floyd picks up the phone.

FLOYD

Hello?

He puts his hand over the receiver.

Dick, it's for you. You here?

DICK

No. I left.

He starts to close the door then opens it again.

I'll take it.
> (*he takes the receiver*)

Hello.
> (*pause*)

Hi, Catherine, I was just walkin' out the –
> (*pause*)

Really?
> (*pause*)

I don't believe it.
> (*pause*)

She really said that?
> (*pause*)

I'll be by first thing.
> (*pause*)

No, thank you for sending me out.
> (*pause*)

Bye, bye.

He hangs up and looks at Clarence.

> (*stunned*)

I got the part on *T. J. Hooker.*

CLARENCE

No shit? Dick, that's great!

Clarence and Alabama are jumping around. Floyd even smiles.

DICK
(*still stunned*)

They didn't even want a callback. They just hired me like that.
Me and Peter Breck are the two heavies. We start shooting
Monday. My call is for seven o'clock in the morning.

CLARENCE

Ah, Dick, let's talk about it in the car. We can't be late.

Dick looks at Clarence. He doesn't want to go.

                              DICK
Clarence.

                              CLARENCE
Yeah?

                              DICK
Um, nothing. Let's go.

They exit.

INT. LAX AIRPORT – HOTEL – DAY

We see the airport and move in closer on a hotel on the landscape.

INT. LAX AIRPORT – HOTEL ROOM – DAY

Lenny can be seen putting a shotgun together. He is sitting on a bed.

Dario enters the frame with his own shotgun. He goes over to Lenny and gives him some shells.

Marvin walks through the frame cocking his own shotgun.

The bathroom door opens behind Lenny and Frankie walks out twirling a couple of .45 automatics in his hands.

INT. BEVERLY WILSHIRE – COPS' HOTEL ROOM – DAY

Nicholson and Dimes and four Detectives from internal affairs are in a room on the same floor as Donowitz. They have just put a wire on Elliot.

                              NICHOLSON
OK, say something.

                              ELLIOT
                      (*talking loud into the wire*)
Hello! Hello! Hello! How now brown cow!

                              DIMES
Just talk regular.

ELLIOT

(*normal tone*)

'But, soft! what light through yonder window breaks?
It is the east and Juliet is the sun.
Arise, fair sun, and kill the envious moon,
Who is already sick and pale with grief – '

NICHOLSON

Are you getting this shit?

DETECTIVE BY TAPE MACHINE

Clear as a bell.

Nicholson, Dimes, and the head IA Officer, Wurlitzer, huddle by Elliot.

DIMES

Now, remember, we'll be monitoring just down the hall.

ELLIOT

And if there's any sign of trouble you'll come in.

NICHOLSON

Like gang-busters. Now, remember, if you don't want to go to
jail, we gotta put your boss in jail.

DIMES

We have to show in court that, without a doubt, a successful man,
an important figure in the Hollywood community, is also dealing
cocaine.

NICHOLSON

So you gotta get him to admit on tape that he's buying this coke.

WURLITZER

And this fellow Clarence?

ELLIOT

Yeah, Clarence.

WURLITZER

You gotta get him to name the police officer behind all this.

ELLIOT

I'll try.

DIMES

You do more than try.

NICHOLSON

You do.

DIMES

Hope you're a good actor, Elliot.

INT. MOVING RED MUSTANG – DAY

Clarence, Dick, and Alabama en route.

DICK

You got that playing basketball?

ALABAMA

Yeah. I got elbowed right in the eye. And if that wasn't enough, I got hurled the ball when I'm not looking. Wham! Right in my face.

They stop at a red light. Clarence looks at Alabama.

CLARENCE

Red light means love, baby.

He and Alabama start kissing.

INT. MOVING CADILLAC – DAY

Marvin, Frankie, Lenny, and Dario in a rented Caddy.

INT. BEVERLY WILSHIRE PARKING LOT – DAY

Clarence, Alabama, and Dick get out of the Mustang. Dick takes the suitcase.

CLARENCE

I'll take that. Now, remember, both of you, let me do the talking.

Clarence takes out his .45. Dick reacts. They walk and talk.

DICK

What the fuck did you bring that for?

CLARENCE

In case.

DICK

In case of what?

CLARENCE

In case they try to kill us. I don't know, what do you want me to say?

DICK

Look, Dillinger, Lee Donowitz is not a pimp –

CLARENCE

I know that, Richard. I don't think I'll need it. But something this last week has taught me, it's better to have a gun and not need it than to need a gun and not have it.

Pause. Clarence stops walking.

Hold it, guys. I don't know about the rest of you, but I'm pretty scared. What say we forget the whole thing.

Dick and Alabama are both surprised and relieved.

DICK

Do you really mean it?

CLARENCE

No, I don't really mean it. Well, I mean, this is our last chance to think about it. How 'bout you, Bama?

ALABAMA

I thought it was what you wanted, Clarence.

CLARENCE

It is what I want. But I don't want to spend the next ten years in jail. I don't want you guys to go to jail. We don't know what could be waiting for us up there. It'll probably be just what it's supposed to be. The only thing that's waiting for us is two hundred thousand dollars. I'm just looking at the downside.

DICK

Now's a helluva time to play 'what if.'

CLARENCE

This is our last chance to play 'what if.' I want to do it. I'm just scared of getting caught.

ALABAMA

It's been fun thinking about the money but I can walk away from it, honey.

CLARENCE

That rhymes.

He kisses her.

DICK

Well, if we're not gonna do it, let's just get in the car and get the fuck outta here.

CLARENCE

Yeah, let's just get outta here.

The three walk back to the car. Clarence gets behind the wheel. The other two climb in. Clarence hops back out.

I'm sorry, guys, I gotta do it. As petrified as I am, I just can't walk away. I'm gonna be kicking myself in the ass for the rest of my life if I don't go in there. Lee Donowitz isn't a gangster lookin' to skin us, and he's not a cop, he's a famous movie producer lookin' to get high. And I'm just the man who can get him there. So what say we throw caution to the wind and let the chips fall where they may.

Clarence grabs the suitcase and makes a beeline for the hotel. Dick and Alabama exchange looks and follow.

INT. BEVERLY WILSHIRE – LOBBY – DAY

Elliot's walking around the lobby. He's very nervous, so he's singing to himself.

ELLIOT
(*singing*)

There's a man who leads a life of danger.
To everyone he meets

he stays a stranger.
Be careful what you say,
you'll give yourself away . . .

INT. BEVERLY WILSHIRE – COPS' HOTEL ROOM – DAY

Nicholson, Dimes, Wurlitzer, and the three other Detectives surround the tape machine. Coming from the machine:

> ELLIOT'S VOICE
> *(off)*

. . . odds are you won't live
to see tomorrow,
Secret agent man,
Secret agent man . . .

Nicholson looks at Dimes.

> NICHOLSON

Why, all of sudden, have I got a bad feeling?

BACK TO: LOBBY

Clarence enters the lobby alone, he's carrying the suitcase. He spots Elliot and goes in his direction. Elliot sees Clarence approaching him. He says to himself, quietly:

> ELLIOT

Elliot, your motivation is to stay out of jail.

Clarence walks up to Elliot, they shake hands.

Where's everybody else?

> CLARENCE

They'll be along.

Alabama and Dick enter the lobby, they join up with Clarence and Elliot.

> ELLIOT

Hi, Dick.

> DICK

How you doin', Elliot?

                    CLARENCE
Well, I guess it's about that time.

                    ELLIOT
I guess so. Follow me.

INT. BEVERLY WILSHIRE – ELEVATOR – DAY

The four of them are riding up in the elevator. As luck would have it, they have the car to themselves. Rinky-dink elevator Muzak is playing. They are all silent. Clarence breaks the silence.

                    CLARENCE
Elliot.

                    ELLIOT
Yeah?

                    CLARENCE
Get on your knees.

Not sure he heard him right.

                    ELLIOT
What?

Clarence hits the stop button on the elevator panel and whips out his .45.

                    CLARENCE
I said, get on your fuckin' knees!

Elliot does it immediately. Dick and Alabama react.

Shut up, both of you, I know what I'm doin'!

BACK TO: COPS' HOTEL ROOM

Pandemonium.

                    DIMES
He knows.

                    NICHOLSON
How the fuck could he know?

DIMES

He saw the wire.

NICHOLSON

How's he supposed to see the wire?

DIMES

He knows something's up.

NICHOLSON

He's bluffing. He can't know.

BACK TO: ELEVATOR

Clarence puts the .45 against Elliot's forehead.

CLARENCE

You must think I'm pretty stupid, don't you?

No answer.

Don't you?

ELLIOT
(*petrified*)

No.

CLARENCE
(*yelling*)

Don't lie to me, motherfucker. You apparently think I'm the
dumbest motherfucker in the world! Don't you? Say: Clarence,
you are without a doubt, the dumbest motherfucker in the whole
wide world. Say it!

BACK TO: COPS

DIMES

We gotta get him outta there.

NICHOLSON

Whatta we gonna do? He's in an elevator.

BACK TO: ELEVATOR

CLARENCE

Say it, goddamn it!

III

ELLIOT

You are the dumbest person in the world.

CLARENCE

Apparently I'm not as dumb as you thought I am.

ELLIOT

No. No you're not.

CLARENCE

What's waiting for us up there. Tell me or I'll pump two right in your face.

BACK TO: COPS

NICHOLSON

He's bluffing ya, Elliot. Can't you see that? You're an actor, remember, the show must go on.

DIMES

This guy's gonna kill him.

BACK TO: ELEVATOR

CLARENCE

Stand up.

Elliot does. The .45 is still pressed against his forehead.

Like Nick Carter used to say: If I'm wrong, I'll apologize. I want you to tell me what's waitin' for us up there. Something's amiss. I can feel it. If anything out of the ordinary goes down, believe this, you're gonna be the first one shot. Trust me. I am AIDS, you fuck me, you die. Now quit making me mad and tell me why I'm so fucking nervous!

BACK TO: COPS

NICHOLSON

He's bluffin', I knew it. He doesn't know shit.

DIMES

Don't blow it, Elliot. He's bluffin'. He just told you so himself.

NICHOLSON

You're an actor, so act, motherfucker.

BACK TO: ELEVATOR

Elliot still hasn't answered.

CLARENCE

OK.

With the .45 up against Elliot's head Clarence puts his palm over the top of the gun to shield himself from the splatter. Alabama and Dick can't believe what he's gonna do.

Elliot, tears running down his face, starts talking for the benefit of the people at the other end of the wire. He sounds like a little boy.

ELLIOT

I don't wanna be here. I wanna go home. I wish somebody would just come and get me 'cause I don't like this. This is not what I thought it would be. And I wish somebody would just take me away. Just take me away. Come and get me. 'Cause I don't like this anymore. I can't take this. I'm sorry but I just can't. So, if somebody would just come to my rescue, everything would be all right.

BACK TO: COPS

Nicholson and Dimes shake their heads. They have a 'well, that's that' expression on their faces.

BACK TO: ELEVATOR

Clarence puts down the gun and hugs Elliot.

CLARENCE

Sorry, Elliot. Nothing personal. I just hadda make sure you're all right. I'm sure. I really apologize for scaring you so bad, but believe me, I'm just as scared as you. Friends?

Elliot, in a state of shock, takes Clarence's hand. Dick and Alabama are relieved.

BACK TO: COPS

Nicholson and Dimes listen open-mouthed, not believing what they're hearing.

INT. DICK'S APARTMENT – DAY

Floyd still lying on the couch watching TV. He hasn't moved since we last saw him.

There is a knock from the door.

> FLOYD
> *(not turning away from TV)*

It's open.

The front door flies open and the four Wise-guys rapidly enter the room. The door slams shut. All have their sawed-offs drawn and pointing at Floyd.

> FLOYD

Yes.

> LENNY

Are you Dick Ritchie?

> FLOYD

No.

> LENNY

Do you know a Clarence Worley?

> FLOYD

Yes.

> LENNY

Do you know where we can find him?

> FLOYD

He's at the Beverly Wilshire.

> LENNY

Where's that?

> FLOYD

Well, you go down Beechwood . . .

INT. BEVERLY WILSHIRE – LEE'S HOTEL ROOM– DAY

CU – A fist knocking on a door.

The door opens and reveals an extremely muscular guy with an Uzi strapped to his shoulder standing in the doorway, his name is Monty.

MONTY

Hi, Elliot. Are these your friends?

ELLIOT

You could say that. Everybody, this is Monty.

MONTY

C'mon in. Lee's in the can. He'll be out in a quick.

They all move into the room, it is very luxurious.

Another incredibly muscular guy, Boris, is sitting on the sofa, he too has an Uzi. Monty begins patting everybody down.

Sorry, nothing personal.

He starts to search Clarence. Clarence backs away.

CLARENCE

No need to search me, daredevil. All you'll find is a .45 calibre automatic.

Boris gets up from the couch.

BORIS

What compelled you to bring that along?

CLARENCE

The same thing that compelled you, Beastmaster, to bring rapid-fire weaponry to a business meeting.

BORIS

I'll take that.

CLARENCE

You'll have to.

The toilet flushes in the bathroom. The door swings open and Lee Donowitz emerges.

LEE

They're here. Who's who?

ELLIOT

Lee, this is my friend Dick, and these are his friends, Clarence
and Alabama.

BORIS
(*pointing at Clarence*)

This guy's packin'.

LEE

Really?

CLARENCE

Well, I have to admit, walkin' through the door and seein' these
Soldier of Fortune poster boys made me a bit nervous. But, Lee,
I'm fairly confident that you came here to do business, not to be a
wise-guy. So, if you want, I'll put the gun on the table.

LEE

I don't think that'll be necessary. Let's all have a seat. Boris, why
don't you be nice and get coffee for everybody.

*They all sit around a fancy glass table except for Boris, who's getting the
coffee, and Monty, who's standing behind Lee's chair.*

CLARENCE

Oh, Mr Donowitz –

LEE

Lee, Clarence. Please don't insult me. Call me Lee.

CLARENCE

OK, sorry, Lee. I just wanna tell you that *Comin' Home in a Body
Bag* is one of my favourite movies. After *Apocalypse Now* I think
it's the best Vietnam movie ever.

LEE

Thank you very much, Clarence.

CLARENCE

You know, most movies that win a lot of Oscars, I can't stand.
Sophie's Choice, Ordinary People, Kramer vs. Kramer, Gandhi. All
that stuff is safe, geriatric, coffee-table dog shit.

LEE

I hear you talkin', Clarence. We park our cars in the same
garage.

CLARENCE

Like that Merchant–Ivory clap-trap. All those assholes make are
unwatchable movies from unreadable books.

*Boris starts placing clear-glass coffee cups in front of everybody and fills
everybody's cup from a fancy coffee pot that he handles like an expert.*

LEE

Clarence, there might be somebody somewhere that agrees with
you more than I do, but I wouldn't count on it.

Clarence is on a roll and he knows it.

CLARENCE

They ain't plays, they ain't books, they certainly ain't movies,
they're films. And do you know what films are? They're for
people who don't like movies. *Mad Max*, that's a movie. *The
Good, the Bad, and the Ugly*, that's a movie. *Rio Bravo*, that's a
movie. *Rumble Fish*, that's a fuckin' movie. And, *Comin' Home
in a Body Bag*, that's a movie. It was the first movie with balls to
win a lot of Oscars since *The Deer Hunter*.

BACK TO: COPS

They're all listening to this.

DIMES

What's this guy doin'? Makin' a drug deal or gettin' a job on the
New Yorker?

BACK TO: LEE'S ROOM

CLARENCE

My uncle Roger and uncle Cliff, both of which were in Nam,
saw *Comin' Home in a Body Bag* and thought it was the most
accurate Vietnam film they'd ever seen.

LEE

You know, Clarence, when a veteran of that bullshit war says
that, it makes the whole project worthwhile. Clarence, my

117

friend, and I call you my friend because we have similar interests, let's take a look at what you have for me.

BACK TO: COPS

NICHOLSON

Thank God.

BACK TO: LEE

Clarence puts the suitcase on the table.

CLARENCE

Lee, when you see this you're gonna shit.

BACK TO: LOBBY

The four Wise-guys are at the desk.

LENNY
(*quietly to the others*)

What was the Jew-boy's name?

MARVIN

Donowitz, he said.

FRONT-DESK GUY

How can I help you, gentlemen?

LENNY

Yeah, we're from Warner Bros. What room is Mr Donowitz in?

BACK TO: LEE

Lee's looking over the cocaine and sampling it.

CLARENCE

Now that's practically uncut. You could, if you so desire, cut it a helluva lot more.

LEE

Don't worry, I'll desire. Boris, could I have some more coffee.

CLARENCE

Me too, Boris.

Boris fills both of their cups. They both, calm as a lake, take cream and sugar. All eyes are on them. Lee uses light cream and sugar, he begins stirring his cup. Clarence uses very heavy cream and sugar.

> LEE
> (*stirring loudly*)
> You like a little coffee with your cream and sugar?

> CLARENCE
> I'm not satisfied till the spoon stands straight up.

Both are cool as cucumbers.

> LEE
> I have to hand it to you, this is not nose garbage, this is quality. Can Boris make anybody a sandwich? I got all kinds of sandwich shit from Canters in there.

> ALABAMA
> No thank you.

> DICK
> No. But thanks.

> CLARENCE
> No thanks, my stomach's a little upset. I ate somethin' at a restaurant that made me a little sick.

> LEE
> Where'd you go?

> CLARENCE
> A Norms in Van Nuys.

> LEE
> Bastards. That's why I always eat at Lawreys.

Lee continues looking at the merchandise.

Alabama writes something on her napkin with a pencil. She slides the napkin over to Clarence. It says: 'You're so cool' with a tiny heart drawn on the bottom of it. Clarence takes the pencil and draws an arrow through the heart. She takes the napkin and puts it in her pocket.

Lee looks up.

OK, Clarence, the merchandise is perfect. But, whenever I'm offered a deal that's too good to be true, it's because it's a lie. Convince me you're on the level.

BACK TO: COPS

NICHOLSON

If he don't bite, we ain't got shit except possession.

DIMES

Convince him.

BACK TO: LEE

CLARENCE

Well, Lee, it's like this. You're getting the bargain of a lifetime because I don't know what the fuck I'm doing. You're used to dealin' with professionals. I'm not a professional. I'm a rank amateur. I could take that, and I could cut it, and I could sell it a little bit at a time, and make a helluva lot more money. But, in order to do that, I'd have to become a drug dealer. I'm not a drug dealer. And I don't want to be a drug dealer. Deal with cut-throat junkies, killers, worry about getting busted all of the time. Just meeting you here today scares the shit outta me, and you're not a junkie, a killer or a cop, you're a fucking movie-maker. I like you, and I'm still scared. I'm a punk kid who picked up a rock in the street, only to find out it's the Hope Diamond. It's worth a million dollars, but I can't get a million dollars for it. But, you can. So, I'll sell it to you for a couple a hundred thousand. You go to make a million. It's all found money to me anyway. Me and my wife are minimum wage kids, two hundred thousand is the world.

LEE

Elliot tells me you're fronting for a dirty cop.

CLARENCE

Well, Elliot wasn't supposed to tell you anythin'.
(*to Elliot*)
Thanks a lot, bigmouth. I knew you were a squid the moment I laid eyes on you. In my book, buddy, you're a piece of shit.

(to Lee)

He's not a dirty cop, he's a good cop. He just saw his chance and he took it.

> **LEE**
>
> Why does he trust you?

> **CLARENCE**
>
> We grew up together.

> **LEE**
>
> If you don't know shit, why does he think you can sell it?

> **CLARENCE**
>
> I bullshitted him.

Lee starts laughing.

> **LEE**
>
> That's wild. This fucking guy's a madman. I love it. Marty, go in the other room and get the money.

Clarence, Alabama and Dick exchange looks.

BACK TO: COPS

Nicholson and Dimes exchange looks.

> **DIMES/NICHOLSON**
>
> Bingo!

BACK TO: ELEVATOR

The four Wise-guys are coming up.

BACK TO: LEE

> **LEE**
> *(pointing at Alabama)*
>
> What's your part in this?

> **ALABAMA**
>
> I'm his wife.

> **LEE**
> *(referring to Dick)*
>
> How 'bout you?

                                    DICK
I know Elliot.

                                    LEE
And Elliot knows me. Tell me, Clarence, what department does
your friend work in?

Dick and Alabama panic.

                                  CLARENCE
                          (*without missing a beat*)
Carson County Sheriffs.

BACK TO: COPS

The internal affairs officers high five.

BACK TO: LEE

Monty brings in a briefcase of money and puts it down on the table.

                                    LEE
Wanna count your money?

                                  CLARENCE
Actually, they can count it. I'd like to use the little boys' room.

BACK TO: COPS

They all stand.

                                   DIMES
OK, boys. Let's go get 'em.

INT. BEVERLY WILSHIRE – LEE'S HOTEL ROOM – BATHROOM –
DAY

*Clarence steps inside the bathroom and shuts the door. As soon as it's shut
he starts doing the twist. He can't believe he's pulled it off. He goes to the
toilet and starts taking a piss. He turns and sees Elvis sitting on the sink.*

                                   ELVIS
Clarence, I gotta hand it to ya. You were cooler than cool.

                                  CLARENCE
I was dying. I thought for sure everyone could see it on my face.

ELVIS

All anybody saw was Clint Eastwood drinkin' coffee.

CLARENCE

Can you develop an ulcer in two minutes? Being cool is hard on your body.

ELVIS

Oh, and your line to Charles Atlas in there: 'I'll take that gun', 'You'll have to.'

CLARENCE

That was cool, wasn't it? You know, I don't even know where that came from. I just opened my mouth and it came out. After I said it I thought, that's a cool line, I gotta remember that.

BACK TO: LEE

Everything's just as it was.

Suddenly, Nicholson, Dimes, and the four Detectives break into the room with guns drawn.

NICHOLSON/DIMES

Police! Freeze, you're all under arrest!

Everybody at the table stands up. Boris and Monty stand ready with the Uzis.

NICHOLSON

You two! Put the guns on the floor and back away!

MONTY

Fuck you! All you pigs put your guns on the floor and back away.

LEE

Monty, what are you talking about? Do what they say.

DIMES

This is your last warning! Drop those fuckin' guns!

BORIS

This is your last warning! We could kill all six of ya and ya fuckin' know it! Now get on the floor!

DICK

What the fuck am I doing here?

LEE

Boris! Everybody's gonna get killed! They're cops!

MONTY

So they're cops. Who gives a shit?

BORIS

Lee, something I never told you about me. I don't like cops.

DIMES

OK, let's everybody calm down and get nice. Nobody has to die.
We don't want it, and you don't want it.

LEE

We don't want it.

*The four Wise-guys burst through the door, shotguns drawn, except for
Frankie, who has two .45 automatics, one in each hand.*

Half of the cops spin around.

WURLITZER

Freeze!

LENNY

Who are you guys?

WURLITZER

Police.

DARIO
(to Lenny)

Do we get any extra if we have to kill cops?

BACK TO: BATHROOM

Clarence and Elvis.

CLARENCE

How do you think I'm doin' with Lee?

ELVIS

Are you kiddin'? He loves you.

CLARENCE

You don't think I'm kissin' his ass, do you?

ELVIS

You're tellin' him what he wants to hear, but that ain't the same thing as kissin' his ass.

CLARENCE

I'm not lyin' to him. I mean it. I loved *Comin' Home in a Body Bag*.

ELVIS

That's why it doesn't come across as ass-kissin', because it's genuine, and he can see that.

Elvis fixes Clarence's collar.

ELVIS

I like ya, Clarence. Always have.

BACK TO: LEE

This is a Mexican stand-off if ever there was one. Gangsters on one end with shotguns. Bodyguards with machine-guns on the other. And cops with handguns in the middle.

Dick's ready to pass out.

Alabama's so scared she pees on herself.

For Elliot, this has been the worst day of his life, and he's just about had it.

ELLIOT

Officer Dimes? Officer Dimes.

Dimes looks at Elliot.

This has nothing to do with me anymore. Can I just leave and you guys just settle it by yourselves?

DIMES

Elliot, shut the fuck up and stay put!

LEE
(*to Elliot*)

How did you know his name? How the fuck did he know your name? Why, you fuckin' little piece of shit!

ELLIOT

Lee, understand, I didn't want to –

NICHOLSON

Shut the fuck up!

LEE

Well, I hope you're not planning on acting any time in the next twenty years 'cause your career is over as of now! You might as well burn your SAG card! To think I treated you as a son! And you stabbed me in the heart!

Lee can't control his anger anymore. He grabs the coffee pot off the table and flings hot coffee into Elliot's face. Elliot screams and falls to his knees.

Instinctively, Nicholson shoots Lee twice.

Alabama screams.

Boris lets loose with his Uzi, painting Nicholson red with bullets.

DIMES
(*screaming*)

Cody!!!

Nicholson flies backwards.

Marvin fires his shotgun, hits Nicholson in the back, Nicholson's body jerks back and forth then on to the floor.

Clarence opens the bathroom door.

Dimes hits the ground firing.

A shot catches Clarence in the forehead.

Alabama screams.

Dario fires his sawed-off. It catches Clarence in the chest, hurling him on top of the bathroom sink, smashing the mirror.

It might have been a stand-off before, but once the firing starts everybody either hits the ground or runs for cover.

Dimes, Alabama, Dick, Lenny, an IA Officer and Wurlitzer hit the ground.

Boris dives into the kitchen area.

Monty tips the table over.

Marvin dives behind the sofa.

Dario runs out of the door and down the hall.

With bullets flying this way and that, some don't have time to do anything. Two IA Officers are shot right away.

Frankie takes an Uzi hit. He goes down firing both automatics.

Elliot gets it from both sides.

Alabama is crawling across the floor, like a soldier in war, towards the bathroom.

Clarence, still barely alive, lays on the sink, twitching. He moves and falls off.

Alabama continues crawling.

Marvin brings his sawed-off from behind the sofa and fires. The shotgun blast hits the glass table and Monty. Monty stands up screaming.

The Cops on the ground let loose, firing into Monty.

As Monty gets hit, his finger hits the trigger of the Uzi, spreading fire all over the apartment.

EXT. BEVERLY WILSHIRE — DAY

Cop cars start arriving in twos in front of the hotel.

   BACK TO: GUNFIGHT

Alabama crawling.

The suitcase full of cocaine is by Dick. Dick grabs it and tosses it in the air. Marvin comes from behind the sofa and fires. The suitcase is hit in mid-air. White powder goes everywhere. The room is enveloped in cocaine.

Dick takes this as his cue and makes a dash out the door.

An IA Officer goes after him.

Lenny makes a break for it.

Wurlitzer goes after him but is pinned down by Marvin.

Alabama reaches the bathroom and finds Clarence.

                          ALABAMA
  Sweety?

Clarence's face is awash with blood.

                          CLARENCE
  I . . . I can't see you . . . I've got blood in my eyes . . .

He dies.

Alabama tries to give him mouth-to-mouth resuscitation.

INT. BEVERLY WILSHIRE — HALLWAY — DAY

Dario runs down the hall, right into a cluster of uniformed police.

He fires his shotgun, hitting two, just before the others chop him to ribbons.

INT. BEVERLY WILSHIRE — ANOTHER HALLWAY

The hallway's empty but we hear footsteps approaching fast. Dick comes around the corner, running as if on fire. Then we see the IA Officer turn the same corner.

                       IA OFFICER
                      (*aiming gun*)

  Freeze!

Dick does.

                            DICK
  I'm unarmed!

                       IA OFFICER
  Put your hands on your head, you son of a bitch!

He does. Then, from off-screen, a shotgun blast tears into the IA Officer, sending him into the wall.

Oh shit.

He starts running again and runs out of frame, then Lenny turns the corner and runs down the hall.

Dick runs into the elevator area, he hits the buttons, he's trapped, it's like a box.

Lenny catches up. Dick raises his hands. Lenny aims his sawed-off.

Look, I don't know who you are, but whatever it was that I did to you, I'm so sorry.

Two elevator doors on either side of them open up.

Lenny looks at Dick. He drops his aim and says:

Lotsa luck.

Lenny dives into one elevator car. Dick jumps into the other, just as the doors close.

BACK TO: HOTEL ROOM

The Mexican stand-off has become two different groups of two pinning each other down.

Wurlitzer has Marvin pinned down behind the sofa and Dimes has Boris pinned down in the kitchen.

In the bathroom, Alabama's pounding on Clarence's bloody chest, trying to get his heart started. It's not working. She slaps him hard in the face a couple of times.

Wake up, goddamn it!

Dimes discards his handgun and pulls one of the sawed-off shotguns from the grip of a dead wise-guy.

Boris peeks around the wall to fire.

Dimes lets loose with a blast. A scream is heard.

BORIS
(*off*)

I'm shot! Stop!

DIMES

Throw out your gun, asshole!

The Uzi's tossed out.

Dimes goes to where Wurlitzer is.

DIMES
(*to Marvin*)

OK, black jacket! It's two against one now! Toss the gun and lie face down on the floor or die like all your friends.

The shotgun's tossed out from behind the sofa.

INT. BEVERLY WILSHIRE — ELEVATOR — DAY

Dick's sitting on the ground, he can't believe any of this. The doors open on the fourth floor. He runs out into the hallway.

HALLWAY

He starts trying the room doors for an open one.

DICK

Oh, God, if you just get me outta this I swear to God I'll never fuck up again. Please, just let me get to *T. J. Hooker* on Monday.

He tries a door, it opens.

STEWARDESS'S ROOM — DAY

Dick steps in. Three gorgeous girls are doing a killer aerobics workout to a video on TV. The music is so loud and they're so into their exercises, they don't hear Dick tiptoe behind them and crawl underneath the bed.

LEE'S ROOM

Boris has caught a lot of buckshot, but he'll live. He's lying on the kitchen

130

floor. Dimes stands over him. He has the sawed-off in his hand.

DIMES
Don't even give me an excuse, motherfucker.

Dimes pats him down for other weapons, there are none.

Wurlitzer puts the cuffs on Marvin and sits him down on the couch.

Dimes looks in the bathroom and sees the dead Clarence with Alabama crying over him.

Dimes walks over to Wurlitzer.

DIMES
Everything's under control here.

WURLITZER
Sorry about Nicholson.

DIMES
Me too.

WURLITZER
I'm gonna go see what's goin' on outside.

DIMES
You do that.

Wurlitzer exits. Dimes grabs the phone.

LOBBY

Shotgun in hand, Lenny moves hurriedly down the lobby.

A Cop yells out.

COP
You! Stop!

Lenny brings up his sawed-off and lets him have it. Other cops rush forward. Lenny grabs a woman standing by.

LENNY
Get back or I'll blow this bitch's brains to kingdom come!

LEE'S ROOM

Dimes is on the phone talking with the department. Boris is still moaning on the floor. Marvin is sitting on the couch with his hands cuffed behind his back. Alabama is crying over Clarence, then she feels something in his jacket. She reaches in and pulls out his .45 calibre automatic. She wipes her eyes. She holds the gun in her hand and remembers Clarence saying:

CLARENCE
(off)

She's a sixteen-calibre kitten! Equally equipped for killin' an' lovin'! She carried a sawed-off shotgun in her purse, a black belt around her waist, and the white-hot fire of hate in her eyes! Alabama Whitman is Pam Grier! Pray for forgiveness. Rated R . . . for Ruthless Revenge!

Alabama steps out of the bathroom, gun in hand.

Marvin turns his head toward her. She shoots him twice.

Dimes, still on the phone, spins around in time to see her raise her gun. She fires. He's hit in the head and flung to the floor.

She sees Boris on the kitchen floor.

ALABAMA

Bye bye, Boris. Good luck.

BORIS

You too, cutie.

She starts to leave and then spots the briefcase full of money. She takes it and walks out the door.

HALLWAY

The elevator opens and Wurlitzer steps out.

Alabama comes around the corner.

WURLITZER

Hey, you!

Alabama shoots him three times in the belly. She steps into the elevator, the doors close.

132

LOBBY

Alabama enters the lobby and proceeds to walk out. In the background, cops are all over the place and Lenny is still yelling with the woman hostage.

LENNY

I wanna car here, takin' me to the airport, with a plane full of gas ready to take me to Kilimanjaro and . . . and a million bucks!
(*pause*)
Small bills!

EXT. BEVERLY WILSHIRE — PARKING LOT — DAY

Alabama puts the briefcase in the trunk. She gets into the Mustang and drives away.

INT. MUSTANG — MOVING — DAY

Alabama's driving fast down the freeway. The DJ on the radio is trying to be funny. She's muttering to herself.

ALABAMA

I could have walked away. I told you that. I told you I could have walked away. This is not my fault. I did not do this. You did this one hundred percent to yourself. I'm not gonna give you the satisfaction of feeling bad. I should laugh 'cause you don't deserve any better. I could get another guy like that. I'm hot lookin'. What are you? Dead! Dumb jerk. Asshole. You're a asshole, you're a asshole, you're a asshole. You wanted it all, didn't ya? Didn't ya? Well whatcha got now? You ain't got the money. You ain't got me. You ain't even got your body anymore. You got nothing'. Nada. Zip. Goose egg. Nil. Donut.

The song 'Little Arrows' by Leapy Lee comes on the radio. Alabama breaks down and starts crying. She pulls the car over to the side. The song continues. She wipes her eyes with a napkin that she pulls out of her jacket. She tosses it on the dashboard. She picks up the .45 and sticks it in her mouth.

She pulls back the hammer. She looks up and sees her reflection in the

133

rear-view mirror. She turns it the other way. She look straight ahead. Her finger tightens on the trigger. She sees the napkin on the dashboard. She opens it up and reads it: 'You're so cool.'

She tosses the gun aside, opens up the trunk, and takes out the briefcase. She looks around for, and finally finds, the Sgt Fury *comic book* Clarence bought her.

And with comic book in one hand, and briefcase in the other, Bama walks away from the Mustang forever.

Leabharlann
Chontae na Mí